HONESTLY ABE

A Cartoon Biography of Abraham Lincoln

(A Revised and Extended Edition)

by
Charles L. Brame

Illustrated by
Edgar "Sol" Soller

**ABE Press, Alta Loma, CA**

HONESTLY ABE
A Cartoon Biography of Abraham Lincoln
by Charles Brame

 ABE Press

Post Office Box 521
Alta Loma, California 91701-0521

CCN: 99-96571

            Publisher's Cataloging-in-Publication
            (Provided by Quality Books, Inc.)

Brame, Charles L.
        Honestly Abe: a cartoon biography of Abraham
        Lincoln / by Charles L. Brame; illustrated by
        Edgar "Sol" Soller. -- 2nd rev and extended ed.
        p. cm.
        Includes bibliographical reference and index.
         ISBN: 0-9659919-3-8 (hbk.)
         ISBN: 0-9659919-1-1 (pbk.)

    1. Lincoln, Abraham, 1809-1865--Caricatures and cartoons.
    2. Lincoln, Abraham, 1809-1865--Philosophy. 3. Lincoln, Abraham, 1809-1865--Biography.
     I. Soller, Edgar. II. Title.

E457.63.B65 2000   973.7'022'2

                              QBI99-1475

299 - 4275

"Abe Lincoln makes all of us smile, feel good, think right, and become instantaneously a little wiser. This book inspires you to bring out the Abe Lincoln in yourself. You will love this book as I do, and you will read it again and again."

Mark Victor Hansen

Co-author, New York Times #1 Best-selling *Chicken Soup for the Soul.*

"Charles Brame and Edgar Soller have joined in presenting a marvelous portrait of Abraham Lincoln. By taking some of his most profound and most persuasive comments, they have provided us with an unforgettable Lincoln. With Lincoln's words, selected by Brame and appropriate cartoons by Soller, there is little more one could ask."

John Hope Franklin, James B Duke Professor of History, Duke University, author of *From Slavery to Freedom*

"This is a book that Lincoln himself would have enjoyed. One can well imagine him showing these cartoons to his cabinet to ease the tension of the Civil War."

John F. Marszalek

William L. Giles Distinguished Professor of History, Mississippi State University, and author of *Sherman, A Soldier's Passion for Order*

"An original and most amusing way to view Abraham Lincoln, either as an introduction or as a reminder of the Lincolnian qualities that too many modern Americans take for granted."

Harold Holzer

Vice Chairman of Lincoln Forum and author of 12 books on Lincoln including *Dear Mr. Lincoln* and *The Lincoln Douglas Debates"*

"Charles Brame and Edgar Soller have provided a simple yet appealing way to understand Abraham Lincoln and his times."

Paul Simon

United States Senator, Director Southern Illinois Public Policy Institute, and Author of *Lincoln's Preparation for Greatness*

"*Honestly Abe A Cartoon Biography of Abraham Lincoln* by Charles Brame, with drawings by Edgar Soller, is a book to delight every Lincoln lover from under 8 to over 80... Here is Lincoln's humor, and Lincoln's gravity, faithfully represented. No coffee table should be without a copy."

Harry Jaffa
Salvatori Research Professor of Political Philosophy emeritus at Claremont McKenna College and author of Lincoln classic *Criss of the House Divided.*

"I have read Brame's *Honestly Abe.* It is very clever, historically valid, and a joy to read. I recommend it."

Alan Nolan, author
of *The Iron Brigade*

"*Honestly Abe* is a delightful book. Merle and I have truly enjoyed reading it. I plan to leave it on the coffee table the next time our grand children come to California for a visit. I know they will like both the illustrations and the stories...(also)..It has a host of sermon illustrations!(for ministers)

Robert (Bob) Edgar
President Claremont School of Theology
and Six term Congressman.

"I find *Honestly Abe* a delightful collection of Lincoln anecdotes and shrewd insights. Combined with adroit cartoon art, this volume makes an ideal introduction to Lincoln for young adults ... , and also provides much food for thought for their elders. I recommend it with enthusiasm."

Roger Fisher
Professor of History, University of Minnesota-Duluth. Author of *Them Damned Pictures: Explorations in American Political Cartoon Art* (1996)

"I think *(Honestly Abe)* is a very clever way to discuss Lincoln's career."

William Gienapp
Professor of History at Harvard University

"Charles Brame has created an innovative way (to) spark conversations about our most famous president. Using the familiar format of political cartooning, he has invented a new genre of historical political cartooning—that is cartoons drawn in the present about past events. Supplying supplementary explanations for each cartoon helps Lincoln scholars and amateurs alike get the point in each instance. Going through *Honestly Abe* is a painless way to become more familiar not only with Lincoln but with a significant era in our history as well."

Ward M. McAfee, Professor of History
California State University-San Bernardino,
Author: *Religion,Race, and Reconstruction:
The Public School in the Politics of the 1870s,*

Excellent rating by Los Angeles City Schools Library Review Committee

CONTENTS

INTRODUCTION

*H*ONESTLY ABE, A Cartoon Biography of Abraham Lincoln is a "fun" book about a funny man who used his humor to sustain our nation and himself through its greatest crisis, the Civil War. Abe Lincoln was the first and greatest humorist to occupy the White House. His humor, like many of his other firsts in that office, was frequently criticized, misunderstood and considered to be in poor taste by many of his contemporaries. But time and history have been kind to Old Abe, and most of us cannot visualize the man without his humor. Many years after Abe Lincoln's untimely murder, men and women who had known him in Illinois would wistfully say, "Gosh, wasn't he funny?" And funny as he was, none of his pictures reveal that humor, that mischievous smile, the impish grin, that warmth and friendliness for which he was known and has been remembered. The attractively drawn cartoons will restore many of the omissions of the photographer—the smile, the warmth and the impish grin.

Most of the events treated in this book rely on humor, but the approach is a bit different from Abe's. Instead of saying."That reminds me of a story," the author responds with, "That reminds me of a cartoon." Since Abe's proverbial jokes and stories inspired laughter and a deeper understanding, the cartoon is designed to accomplish the same ends.

For the sake of clarity and ease in interpretation, present-day symbols, vocabulary, and techniques are utilized. Popular terms, even slang, appear. Modern gadgetry, such as closed circuit TV cameras, are included. Charlie B appears as the aide that all successful politicians and other persons of great power believe they must have—a spin doctor: The slick public relations man whose duty it is to create images and to win for his clients. His purpose is to convince the public that what appears to be the truth really is the truth. Honestly, there never was a Charlie B in the Lincoln administration, but he appears in this work to create comic interest, to be a straight man for Old Abe and occasionally to be the recipient of the Rail Splitter's best barbs. However, Charlie B is a little different from most current spin doctors: He actually desires to present the truth, serves without pay and genuinely cares for his boss and the other people who care about his boss. While observing and laughing at Charlie B and with Abe Lincoln, we may be better able to see what is actually happening to us today. If we do, we might think more and wonder why we are laughing.

As we continue to delve into this study of Abe Lincoln, we will rediscover from these pages that he was a prolific writer of excellent prose and speeches. Abe is our greatest writing president, and he produced more words than his favorite author, William Shakespeare. The Gettysburg and Second Inaugural addresses are two of the greatest ever crafted. Lord Curzon, Chancellor of the University of Oxford, pronounced them two of the three supreme masterpieces of

English eloquence. Both contain phrases that are known by almost every English speaking adult, and many parts are familiar to knowledgeable individuals throughout the rest of the world. The Gettysburg Address is probably the most popular prose in all of man's history.

There are scholars who believe that if Lincoln had never been President of the United States, he still would have become one of the great writers of his age. However, I do not agree. Abe was a political animal, and in his frame of reference, politics was inclusive of all of man's activities[1]. It was Abe's involvement with politics that made him an Illinois figure, caught the eye of the nation's public and proclaimed him a worldwide personality. With his masterful handling of the nation during the Civil War and the freeing of the slaves, Lincoln endeared himself to international memory. He used the presidency as a bully platform to minister to the world and to make it a little more humane. This has created the lasting interest in the man and his writings.

Our journey will reveal that in spite of his clear delivery, unique style, brevity and colorful metaphors, Abe was misunderstood and frequently quoted out of context from his time to the present. Two years after he had delivered his "Half Slave—Half Free Speech," he was still being asked, "What did you mean, Mr. Lincoln?" In frustration he wrote, "I meant all I said, and did not mean anything I did not say[2]." Abe and his aide, Charlie B, will graphically explain the "...did not mean what I did not say."

We will find Abe at his funniest when he responds to partisan debate and heckling. When a badgering, stump politician yelled from the audience, "I just don't understand your speeches, Lincoln," Abe laughingly replied, "There are always some fleas a hound dog just can't get to."

The reader will be amazed to learn that a school of recent scholars known as revisionists has accused Abe of being an ambitious, power hungry Caesar or Napoleon. They justify their position on his famous Young Men's Lyceum Speech, given when he was only twenty-eight. Furthermore, many of them contend that he was not much of a leader in saving the Union or in freeing the slaves, and they try to neutralize his impact on many of his other great accomplishments. The cartoon rebuttal to these revisionists is clear and laughable. Abe would certainly enjoy the author's response.

The sources of Abe's wit and humor will be revealed. Most of his material was second hand. When asked if he originated his stories, he responded that they came from far better story tellers than he. "I'm just a 're-teller' and not a wholesaler of stories," he remarked. The answer reveals another of his techniques: The deliberate misspelling and mispronouncing of words to create laughter and to provoke thought. Those who believed Abe was too ignorant to realize he was making a mistake vastly underestimated this clever man's humor.

For thirty-three years I taught high school and junior college history and political science courses and enjoyed almost every moment of it. I am a serious student of history and a strong believer in "the anecdote is the antidote to boredom." As a result, I was constantly digging up amusing and truthful incidents about the lives of great people and inventing unique ways to present them to students. Charlie B and re-enacting Abraham Lincoln were products of that approach to teaching and led to a retirement career as a professional Abraham Lincoln look-a-like, actor and writer.

During the past twenty-five years, in addition to my movie and TV work, I have successfully presented nearly twenty-six hundred one man shows and speeches as Abraham Lincoln throughout a large part of the United States. All of the material in this book is a result of this multi-careered experience and has been thoroughly tested by audiences. At the conclusion of these productions, members of the audience have consistently said they never knew how much Old Abe had done. Many would then say, "You ought to write a book. If you wrote one like you tell it, I'd buy it."

Honestly, I cannot write it like I tell it. An actor conveys a vast amount of feeling and information to the audience through body language, inflection of voice, tone, costuming and the atmosphere of the stage and auditorium. Therefore, in endeavoring to recreate the same effect, *Honestly Abe* substitutes the nuances and devices of the artist for the dramatic techniques of the actor.

Like Abe's and Charlie B's fathers used to say, "There is many a truth told in jest." This is a nonfiction book which tells the truth, but with a twist: A twist of humor, a twist of religion, a twist of philosophy, a twist of history, a twist of ....? It is not intended to be a scholarly, historical biography. Within its jestful truth there are moments of sadness and tears that cannot be avoided. But in the end, may the reader find it hard to distinguish the tears of pain from those of the joy induced by laughter.

Sincerely,

Charles Brame

1. To a majority of mankind the term politician is a word of opprobrium while statesman is just fine. Harry Truman used to say, "Everybody dislikes politicians and admires statesmen. I like politicians and most of them do a great job. Besides, a statesman ain't noth'n but a dead politician."

2. Wit and Wisdom, 76. Letter to O .P. Hall, J. R. Fullenwider & U. F. Correll, 02/14/60.

MORE HONESTLY ABE

Since its publication, Honestly Abe has received the recognition of publishers, historians, educators, ministers, and just plain folks. The Publishers' Marketing Association, an association of 3300 independent publishers, presented the book the prestigious Benjamin Franklin Award for Biography in 1999-a rare accomplishment for a first time author and publisher. The library committee of the second largest school district in the nation gave it an excellent rating and a priority one to buy as a reference book for its libraries. The president of a great school of theology personally enjoyed the book and said it had many useful illustrations for ministers to use as ideas for sermons. The endorsements of many top Lincoln historians and authors have been gratefully received. Finally, the unsolicited praise of plumbers, mothers, janitors, etc., has been a delight, reenforcing our conviction that Honestly Abe makes history enjoyable and useful.

The acceptance by the book's readers and owners has been a daily joy and a source of enlightenment. Comments prove that Honestly Abe is a unique book, as the author intended to be. A prominent scholar and professor of history declared that the author has invented a new genre of political cartoons. Another expert on political cartoons enthusiastically recommended it as a clever book that was great for young adults and food for thought for their elders. It has had a great circulation rate at libraries, and kids in school like it so much that they keep it too long. Couples have reported enjoying a page or two of the book with their breakfasts, and a number of parents are reading favorite selections to their children, proof that Honestly Abe is a book for adults which can also be enjoyed by children.

A few well intended, critical comments have been received, and the author has responded. Some suggested the need of a glossary to explain archaic words and colloquial phrases popular in Lincoln's day as well as to elaborate on historical events of the era. A glossary has been introduced. Some of the commentaries and cartoons were vague and needed fine tuning. They have been either redrawn or rewritten. Also, a list of popular web sites has been added to the bibliography. In the second edition, the author has chosen to include additional events, bits of Abe's writings, or important contributions. Finally, the choice of the word expose' in the sub-title has been revised to read, *A Cartoon Biography of Abraham Lincoln*. This revised edition is presented, hoping to make *Honestly Abe* an even more enjoyable and useful volume for you, our beloved readers.

ACKNOWLEDGMENTS

This is a political cartoon biography of Abraham Lincoln. To the best of my knowledge, there has never been a book of this kind about Lincoln. Each page contains a cartoon about a quote or an event in his life and an editorial commentary. The format required a tremendous amount of art work, desktop publishing and editorial help to augment the writing. While many persons helped, the contributions of three very special people stand out.

It has been a delight and a terrific growth experience to have worked with award winning Edgar Soller, a great artist and editorial cartoonist. For years he drew for Hanna Barbera Productions, and his political cartoons have been in Pelican Publishing's *Best of Editorial Cartoons Of The Year* regularly since the early seventies. I am thankful that he valued my concept and material enough to participate in this endeavor. He has remained constant in his commitment to the book. Furthermore, I admire and respect his integrity, conviction and dedication to his principles. As a young man he was forced to flee his native land rather than face imprisonment and possibly death because of his artistic expression. As usual, the government paid little attention to the editors of the newspapers but was most concerned about the cartoonist.

The contribution of Craig Richards has been terrific. Since I know little about desktop publishing and was creating a book which required an unusual amount of such expertise, his offer to help was greatly appreciated.

I thank my wife of over forty-five years, Geri. As a live-in spell-checker, punctuation expert, editor and proof reader, she has devoted long hours. Always the loving helpmate, she was a valuable asset and is greatly appreciated.

My readers Baxley Thames, Dr. Danny King ,and Dr. Walter Schuilling were a great help on the first printing. The comments and suggestions of my brother, Dr. Ray Brame, were most helpful as were the suggestions and encouragement of Kim Bauer, historian with the Illinois State Historical Library.

CARTOONS AND COMMENTARY

LIST OF CARTOONS

17. Can't Reach 'Em All
18. Called to Be Abe's Spin Doctor
19. He's Just Beautiful, Pa
20. Abe's Definition of Democracy
21. Will'n Ta Risk the Hog!
22. School by Littles
23. A Lawyer's Creed
24. A Woods Colt?
25. Shakespeare on the Sangamon
26. The Dunghill Lincolns'
27. The Chinfly Lincolns'
28. Dancing in the Worst Way
29. The Know Nothing Know Nothing
30. Mud-Sill Labor
31. Free Labor
32. How Much Is Enough for Membership?
33. He Tempers the Wind
34. The Shorn Lambs
35. Fuller Justice
36. Captain Lincoln's Black Hawk War Experience
37. My Dog's Ready
38. The Starving Jackass
39. Foot Prints on the Ceiling
40. Friend Douglas
41. The Length and Breadth of Illinois Politics
42. Don't Blame Mayme
43. Winking Out of Business
44. Tom's Lost Spirits
45. She Gave Her Love without Reservations
46. The Soap Expert
47. With a Trumpet Voice and a Tin Ear
48. Presidents'
49. Pardons
50. Deliver Us from Proverbs
51. A Strict Judge
52. Three Men in a Bed
53. Good Friends Can Have Vices!
54. Sipping Through the Bunghole
55. Presume the Judge Knows Nothing
56. Book Larnin's Good
57. Abe's Bustin' Out All Under
58. A one Idea Court
59. Reading With Ears; Hearing With Eyes
60. He Might Have Stayed Home
61. Equals Is Equals
62. The innocent Bone of Contention
63. The Sacrificial Prize
64. Spared by the Absence of Appetite
65. More Facts, Less Opinion
66. The Most Words into the Smallest Ideas
67. Every Blade a Study
68. The Dueling Dudes of Springfield
69. And Winning by inches
70. Got Three, Both Want Two
71. Dictating a New Address
72. Jokes by Tom
73. The Ignorant and Vicious Shall Share
74. The Skinniest Horse
75. A Thought at a Time and Shuffling a Line
76. Never Old Enough
77. He Argued His Opponent's Case and Won
78. Cruel and Unusual Punishment
79. The Worst Friend
80. Writing Just Right
81. Abe's Whatyoucallit
82. The Long and the Short of It
83. Become a Slave and Take the Good of It
84. Is a Chestnut Horse a Horse Chestnut?
85. No Grievance Justifies Mob Law
86. A Bad Split Instead of a Strike
87. Out, Out Damned Spot(Ty) Lincoln
88. Keeping It Simple
89. Let 'Em Tear the House Down
90. Special Ability for a Winning Politician
91. A Superior Opportunity to Do Good
92. Old Abe Is Puttin' on (H)Airs
93. Caesar's Hair
94. Whence Come Wealth
95. What to Do With That Hat?
96. In Like Pharaoh
97. Out Like Moses
98. Never Sell Out Old Friends
99. Crossing Fox River
100. Does Your Head Know When Your Feet Get Cold?
101. Surprise Surprise?
102. Lamon, Sing Me a Sad, Sweet Song
103. Honestly, Abe?
104. Abe on Slavery
105. Race and Marriage
106. Abe Signs a Declaration July Fourth
107. For the Man Or the Money
108. Tom Wrote: Abe Acted!
109. The Flo' Through the Grapevine
110. Friend Douglas Hits a Double
111. A Difference Between Being Paid to Eat and Paying for It

LIST OF CARTOONS

LIST OF CARTOONS

CALLED TO BE ABE LINCOLN'S SPIN DOCTOR

It is amazing how experts, disciples and mankind in general can observe the same facts and study the same words and arrive at completely different conclusions. Such has frequently been the case with Abe Lincoln's words. Although our greatest writing president had a lucid, clear style which should be easily understood, his words have frequently been misinterpreted and taken out of context. At times diametrically opposing groups have used the same phrases to justify their causes.

This tendency toward misinterpretation and reading out of context plagued Lincoln before his death. One time in frustration Abe wrote, "I meant all I said and did not mean anything I did not say." It is this "did not mean anything I did not say" usage that mandates a modern day public relations expert known as a spin doctor, and Abe's spin doctor is Charlie B.

CAN'T REACH 'EM ALL

Most of Lincoln's letters, speeches and reported comments are masterpieces of clarity and eloquence. He wanted people from all walks of life to be able to understand and enjoy them. By employing simple and easy to understand words and including many familiar quotes from the Bible and other great literary masterpieces, he was able to accomplish that end.

In spite of this clarity, there were groups and individuals who said they could not understand him, especially in politics. When this happened, Abe usually laughed off their complaints with a shrug and a quip. When a gentleman who opposed his political views said. "I can't understand those speeches of Lincoln," Abe replied, "There are always some fleas a dog just can't reach."

HE'S JUST BEAUTIFUL, PA

Charles Dana spoke of Lincoln's natural and easy grace with children. No child shrank from his presence, and the little ones enjoyed him as they might a trusted horse or pet dog. Abe's face beamed one day, when after bending over and kissing a little girl, she called out to her parents as she skipped out of his White House office, "Why he's only a man after all. Oh, Pa! He isn't ugly at all; he's just beautiful."

ABE'S DEFINITION OF DEMOCRACY

This idea of Democracy was originally expressed in Lincoln's own handwriting in the form of an autograph. Wouldn't we all love to author such a spontaneous note? What better proof that Abe did his own writing and of his sincerity in his belief that democracy and slavery were incompatible?

"As I would not be a slave, so I would not be a master. This expresses my idea of democracy, Whatever differs from this, to the extent of the difference, is no democracy."

WILL'N TA RISK THE HOG!

Today's comedian is a master of the one liner. Delivered in staccato outbursts and frequently off-color, his material is designed to entertain and is not very subtle. Long on shock and short of cerebral stimulation, his product, like the fast food outlet, is dished out quickly, mediocre in quality and bland—apparently what the customer wants.

Abe came from a different time with a different frame of reference. His one liners wouldn't go over today. Being a rural mid 19th century man, his jokes would not be understood by most of the people and would be considered corny and hickish. Often they were a spontaneous, humorous reaction to a particular situation like the following:

Once he was asked by a farmer, "Abe, would you butcher a hog for me?" Abe: "If you're will'n to risk the hog, so am I."
* See ABE'S GOT TO HAVE A BEARD.

SCHOOL BY LITTLES

According to his brief hand written biography, Abe... "went to school by littles. Two or three months here, there, less than a year in all..(and)..when I came of age, I could read, write and cipher to the rule of three". They were blab schools, and the children did not have books to study. Instead they copied their lessons out of the masters' texts and committed them to memory by talking out loud, blabbing, to themselves. The rest of his education was a product of necessity. From his school boy days he continued to memorize literary masterpieces which gave him a fabulous source of beloved quotes to garnish his speeches and writings. From that spotty education he acquired two bad habits which remained with him for the rest of his life.: He could not remember anything he read unless he read it aloud, and he was always talking to himself.

He was most aware of this inadequacy and at times felt insecure, especially when around men who flaunted their good educations. As a result, he wanted others to have a good, practical education. All of his political life he was for education and considered it a function of government. In his very first campaign for office he wrote, "Upon the subject of education...I can only say that I view it as the most important subject which we as a people can be engaged in."

A LAWYER'S CREED

Sometime in 1850, Lincoln prepared his "Notes For A Law Lecture" for young lawyers. It was never given, but the ideals expressed make it worthy of inscription on the walls of every law office, and, if practiced, the professional image of today's lawyers would be much higher. Abe's reputation as a lawyer was proof that he practiced what he preached.

A WOODS COLT?

From his childhood until the present, rumors continue to circulate that Abe Lincoln was an illegitimate, or in old southern slang terms, a woods colt. Gossip in Kentucky made the rounds that mumps or an accidental castration rendered the elder Lincoln impotent. Allegations were made that Chief Justice John Marshall, John C. Calhoun, Abraham Enlow, (at times spelled Inlow,) and others were his father.

A rumor has even circulated that Nancy Hanks was not his mother. In July of 1863, John J. Joel wrote William Seward, Lincoln's Secretary of State, that Abe was the illegiti-mate son of a man by the name of Inlow and a Negress named Hanna Hanks and that the President's "real name was Abraham Hanks."

It is possible that Abe doubted that Thomas Lincoln was his father and that such rumors may have reached his ears when he was a boy in Kentucky. Needless to say, all of them have been proved groundless by reliable, historical scholarship. Tom and Nancy Lincoln had three children early in their marriage, and one of them was Abe Lincoln. Abe was not a woods colt!

SHAKESPEARE ON THE SANGAMON

Much of Lincoln's "spotty" education and his future outlook on life was acquired at New Salem, Illinois. The small village contained many talented, educated and interesting residents: Mentor Graham, the village schoolmaster; Dr. John Allen, village doctor and a Dartmouth College graduate; veterans from the Revolutionary and 1812 Wars; highly skilled craftsman; survivors of the Indian wars; and ministers. All made their mark.

Jack Kelso was the local, alcoholic blacksmith who loved poetry. Abe enjoyed his company. Jack loved to fish, and the two men spent many an hour together on the banks of the Sangamon River. While fishing, Abe caught something of greater importance from Kelso: Shakespeare and Bobby Burns. The Bard of Avon was Abe's favorite writer, and he memorized hundreds of pages from his plays and poems. And the Scot's Plowman's pride of the common man reinforced the Rail Splitter's confidence in himself in spite of his humble origin, for "A Man's A Man And A That And A That."

THE DUNGHILL LINCOLNS

Over the years quite a controversy has existed as to the origin of Abe Lincoln. There are two schools of thought on the subject, and the dispute arose over the influence on Lincoln's life in Indiana. The combatants are known as "dunghillers" and "chin flyers."

The dunghill group has espoused the traditional origin of the Rail Splitter as the product of one of the undistinguished families of the frontier—rough, common folk of questionable ancestry possessing crude values and exhibiting little taste for the refinements of life. In spite of his humble beginnings, Abe rose above these handicaps to become a successful man and the president. Abe believed much of this to be true as stated in a brief autobiography he wrote of his life in 1859. This letter was used as the basis of a campaign article by eastern Republicans to inform the public about their candidate.

THE CHINFLY LINCOLNS

The "chinflyers" maintain that the Lincoln family was rather well to do. Tom Lincoln was a successful frontier farmer who took good care of his family, encouraged his son to get a good education and inspired Abe to make something of himself. Its supporters are mainly Hoosiers from Indiana that felt the "dung-hillers" downplayed the influence of Lincoln's boyhood years in their fair state.

DANCING IN THE WORST WAY

One of the first opportunities Abe had to talk with Miss Mary Todd was at a dance. Being bashful, a very poor dancer and knowing that she was from a distinguished family, he finally got the courage to ask her for a dance. "My dear Miss Todd," he timidly asked, "I would like to dance with you in the worst way." She accepted his offer and quickly discovered that he really meant it. Bruised, battered and suffering pained feet, she told him at the conclusion of the dance, "Mr. Lincoln, you wanted to dance with me in the worst way, and you certainly have achieved your ambition."

In spite of his poor dancing and rough exterior, Miss Todd saw much more in him. After a rather hectic courtship, she married Abe. In time his dancing did improve a little, without the benefit of Arthur Murray. The incident was one of those unique events that every loving couple experiences and never forgets. It is also an event that the people of this country love sharing about their favorite president.

THE KNOW NOTHING KNOW NOTHING

Always afraid of extremism and bigoted movements, Abe once wrote, "As a nation, we began by declaring 'that all men are created equal'. We now practically read it 'all men are created equal, except Negroes'. When the Know Nothings get control, it will read 'all men are created equal, except Negroes, and foreigners, and Catholics.' When it comes to this I should prefer emigrating to some country where they make no pretense of loving liberty—to Russia, for instance, where despotism can be taken pure, and without the base alloy of hypocrisy."

MUD-SILL LABOR

Mud-sills are the lowest timbers or logs of a building's walls. They are made from special wood that resists rot and insect infestation and prevents such damage from spreading to the rest of the wood. Rarely seen and often buried beneath the soil, mud-sills guarantee and sustain the rest of the structure.

Abe Lincoln applied the term to describe a class of workers then existing in many parts of the world. According to him there were two theories about labor: Mud-sill and Free labor. The "Mud-sillers" believed that labor was either to be owned or controlled by capital. It was composed of ignorant and uneducated workers and their families, whose status was perpetual and fatally fixed as slaves, serfs or peasants bound to the land. They existed for the benefit of those who owned or controlled them. Like the building's mud-sills, this labor supported the economy but got little of itsfruits.

In a most vivid way, Abe described the ideal product of those who espoused and profited from this type of labor: "According to this theory, a blind horse upon a treadmill, is a perfect illustration of what a laborer should be— all the better for being blind, that he could not tread out of place or kick understandingly. Such a laborer neither desires nor cares about elevating status, finding comfort in the security provided by those who own it." Old Abe considered this system of labor contemptible and contrary to the ideals expressed in the Declaration of Independence.

FREE LABOR

Abe endorsed and firmly believed in the theory of free labor. It was superior to and the originator of capital. When given the opportunity and education which was indispensable for advancement, free laborers had climbed up the economic ladder by hard work, thrift and prudent planning. Millions of unskilled, toolless men had become farmers, small town businessmen and professionals. Proud of their success, they encouraged and perpetuated the cycle of advancement for other laborers. Free labor was the embryo and the yeast of capitalism.

HOW MUCH IS ENOUGH FOR MEMBERSHIP

During Abe's New Salem days, even the local Baptist Church was not ready to take a stand against whisky. One of its members was Mentor Graham, New Salem school teacher, friend and volunteer tutor to Abe. When he joined the temperance group, he was thrown out of the church. At the same time the deacons suspended another member who was a notorious drunk.

Their collective action puzzled another member. Standing up at the meeting and shaking a half full bottle so all could see, he drawled, "Brethering, you have throw'n out one member because he did not drink, and another 'cause he got drunk, and I wants to know. How much of this 'ere critter does a man have to drink to remain in full membership of this here church?"

HE TEMPERS THE WIND

During the late summer of 1841, Lincoln made a low water steamboat trip from Kentucky to St. Louis. In a letter to Josh Speed's sister, Mary, Abe observed an incident which slaves always feared, and he described it this way."On board were twelve negro men who had been purchased in Kentucky and were being taken to a farm in the deep South. The men were chained six and six together and appeared like so many fish on a trot line. In that condition they were being separated forever from the scenes of their childhood and families and being sent to a place of perpetual slavery where the lash of the master was more ruthless and unrelenting than any other where. And yet, amid all of these distressing circumstances, as we would find them, they appeared to be the most apparently happy creatures on board... they danced, sang, cracked jokes, and played various games at cards...."

H ow true it is that 'God tempers the wind to the shorn lamb,' or in other words, that He renders the worst of human conditions tolerable, while He permits the best, to be nothing better than tolerable."

Abe never forgot that scene and how it impressed him. Years later he restated that event in a letter to Josh Speed, who was probably his dearest friend.

FULLER JUSTICE

The amount and method of payment for service rendered by lawyers has certainly changed from Abe's day. Rarely is a fixed fee for a particular service assessed, and the lawyer's clock runs like the meter on a cab with billable hours the yardstick that makes partners out of associates. Furthermore, a large up front payment is demanded which precludes the average person from securing justice.

It's a far cry from the way Abe advised his young lawyers of the Illinois Bar.

"As a general rule never take your whole fee in advance, nor any more than a small retainer. When fully paid beforehand, you are more than a common mortal if you can feel the same interest in the case, as if something was still in prospect for you, as well as for your client."

CAPTAIN LINCOLN'S BLACK HAWK WAR EXPERIENCE

A be had very little military experience and admitted it. This background caused problems for him, especially when dealing with professional military men. His total military experience consisted of his brief stint in the Black Hawk Indian wars in the early 1830's, in western Illinois. Although he had no military training, he was elected captain of the militia unit from New Salem. The unit had no battlefield experience. When his company was disbanded, he served a couple of more months in the army before returning to New Salem.

He often joked about that experience and frequently described it in comic fashion.

"Oh," he chortled, "I took part in the Indian wars against old Black Hawk. Never saw any Indians, but we had quite a few 'skirmishes' with the 'muskeeters' and raided a few wild onion patches."

**Suckers, the nickname given to persons born and reared in Illinois.

MY DOG'S READY

Harry Truman once said that his most important job was to persuade the person in his administration who had the job to do the job. Abe was faced with the same situation; people in responsible positions did not do what they were supposed to do. He was constantly encouraging, begging, bribing, humoring, threatening, etc. his generals and appointees to get the job done instead of giving reasons for their failure. To inspire them he frequently told this anecdote:

A farmer over Bloomington way had a small bull terrier that was the fight'nest mutt he ever saw. The terrier whipped every dog he tangled with; big ones, little ones, bald headed, cross eyed, he didn't cull anything. One day, a nearby neighbor of the terrier's owner asked, "How come your small dog has whupped ever dog he tangled with in McClean County? My dog's twice as big as yours, and he whupped him too. Ain't it a mystery how he does that?"

The terrier's owner replied, "Oh, there's no mystery to that. You see, your dog, like the others, is half way through the fight before he's ready. My dog's ready!"

THE STARVING JACKASS

So many of Abe's generals and officials couldn't or wouldn't make decisions. He was frustrated with dallying and dawdling. Such behavior reminded him of the hungry donkey left standing in doubt between two stacks of hay who starved to death rather than make a choice.

FOOT PRINTS ON THE CEILING

Hardly a child finishes elementary school in this country without being exposed to the "foot prints on the ceiling" practical joke that Abe played on his beloved stepmother as a teen age youth.

He grew up like a weed eventually reaching nearly six feet four inches in his prime. When Tom Lincoln built his cabin on Little Pigeon Creek, he hadn't planned on his son's tall height and installed the rafters at an average height. As a result, they were too low, and Abe frequently bumped his head on the rafters. His discomfort amused his stepmother, whom he affectionately called Momma Sally. Whenever he forgot about the rafters and whacked his head, her usual response was, "Young man, it's alright to track up my floors. Just don't go track'n up my ceil'ns."

One day, when she was out visiting with a neighbor, Abe got one of the younger boys in the neighborhood to walk bare footed in a mud puddle. He then carried the youth to the cabin, held him upside down and had him walk across the ceiling leaving a line of muddy foot prints. When Momma Sally returned, she made a startling discovery, muddy footprints on her white washed ceiling. She enjoyed being the victim, and another little incident became the grist on which loving relationships are built. The rest is history, and the world loves the result and continues to tell the story.

FRIEND DOUGLAS

Although Abe Lincoln and Stephen Douglas were political enemies for almost twenty-five years, personally they were very good friends. Being lawyers and true believers in the two party system, they understood and appreciated the adversary system of justice and politics. To them it was the necessary and sophisticated ingredient of the democratic process of majority rule and the loyal opposition.

Abe liked to be called Lincoln by his friends, and the rest addressed him as Mr. Lincoln. After Douglas became a Supreme Court Justice in Illinois, Abe addressed him publicly and privately as Judge Douglas. Whenever they had not seen each other for a long period of time, they always shook hands and embraced. One does not need much of an imagination to visualize this rather comic sight of tall, daddy long legs Abe at six feet four bending down to embrace short, portly, rotund bottomed Steve Douglas.

THE LENGTH AND BREADTH OF ILLINOIS POLITICS

For over two decades in Illinois politics, if a group or interest wanted something done by the state government at Springfield, the two persons to see were Stephen Douglas, Democrat, and Abe Lincoln, Whig and later Republican. They were the "Mr. Fix Its" at the state capital.

Whenever they were both in town, being good personal friends, it was a common sight to see them walking down the streets of Springfield arm in arm. Local wits used to say as they passed by, "There goes the length and breadth of Illinois politics."

DON'T BLAME MAYME

Abe did not subscribe to the view that women possessed weak characters and were the cause of man's fall. He did not display the conventional male attitude of the time that women were weak, frail creatures devoid of common sense and strong character. Abe treated them with the same respect accorded men. When women got around him, they quickly detected this attitude and appreciated the homely man who did not look down upon them because they were born women.

This outlook toward women was expressed in the following bit of doggerel he composed as a school youth at Pigeon Creek, Indiana.

"Whatever spiteful fools may say,
Each jealous, ranting yelper,
No woman ever went astray
Without a man to help her."

Abe never considered himself much of a businessman. In his one endeavor of being a merchant he and his partner, William Berry, went bankrupt with their store at New Salem, Illinois. Abe was interested in reading, talking and politicking, and Bill drank too much. So they got deeper in debt, and the store just winked out, leaving Abe saddled with his "national debt".

Although a very talented man, making money in a business just did not appeal to him. Lincoln loved the law and its hand maiden, politics, because he enjoyed serving people. As he said, "I do not have much talent for business, for it appears to me that men who desire just to make money spend too much time thinking about making it. I made my money from the law."

TOM'S LOST SPIRITS

In this country most of us are acquainted with Tom Lincoln and his family's 1816 move from Kentucky to Indiana and how he traded his Knob Creek farm for 10 barrels of whiskey. Also, we learned that during the move he lost his earthly possessions when his flatboat sank, including his whiskey. The only source for this event is minister-schoolmaster, William Thayer's *The Pioneer Boy and How to Become President* printed in the 1880's.

Since Tom Lincoln was a deacon in the Baptist Church, it is highly improbable that he would have tolerated or been involved in that kind of spiritual enterprize. The incident is not cut from whole cloth.

MYTH

SHE GAVE HER LOVE WITHOUT RESERVATIONS

When Abe talked about his Mother, he usually meant his stepmother, Sarah Bush Lincoln. Upon arriving at Pigeon Creek, she changed their lonely, dirty, little cabin into a warm and loving home. "She gave us love," he often remarked, "and we needed love so badly." One of the last things he did before he went to Washington to become President was to visit with her. They loved each other dearly.

Tom Lincoln was not an ignorant or lazy man, but, as Abe said, "He just seemed to have a lot of plain bad luck coupled with bad judgement." When he died, there was nothing left for his widow, and she was practically penniless. Abe bought a farm and gave it to her.

His good friend, lawyer and confidant, Judge David Davis, suggested that he place the property in a living trust, so that no one could take it from her. When she passed away, it would revert to Lincoln. Abe was somewhat incensed at the suggestion and told Davis, "That woman gave me her love without any reservations or conditions when I was a lad and needed it, and that's the way I'm giving her this farm!"

THE SOAP EXPERT

When a manufacturer of soap asked presidential candidate Lincoln for a testimonial for his product, Abe good humoredly complied, quoting his "superior officer" in domestic affairs.

Sept. 26, 1860
Dear Sir:

Some specimens of your Soap have been used at our house, and Mrs. L. declares it is a superior article. She at the same time protests that I have never given sufficient attention to the "soap question" to be a competent judge.

A. Lincoln

WITH A TRUMPET VOICE AND A TIN EAR

Although Abe could not sing or play musical instruments, he had a great love for most kinds of music and was very responsive to it. Three different sources attest to his lack of talent or "tin ear". Dennis Hanks, his older cousin who grew up with him, said that Abe wasn't much of a singer; couldn't even sing "Pore Old Ned," though he tried often enough. His long time partner and dear friend, William Herndon, was once asked if Lincoln could sing. Billie answered the question with a question which is clear and to the point. "Can a jackass whistle?" Finally, Abe always declared in public that he could not sing, but he never gave up trying.

He had no love of the classics but enjoyed everything between early minstrel nonsense songs and popular ballads of his day. His friends knew that he was sentimental and that certain types of ballads brought tears to his eyes. He loved to have his lawyer friend, Ward Lamon, play the banjo and sing such tear jerkers as "Twenty Years Ago," which brought tears every time. On the other hand, he got a big kick out of "None Can Love Like An Irishman."

Much has been written and said of Lincoln's mercy regarding soldiers given death sentences for desertion and related violations of military law. He sought to make the seat of power a seat of mercy and pardoned most of those who were to be shot or hanged for such crimes. He took it upon himself as Commander in Chief to review every court-martial death sentence for desertion and similar crimes. However, little is said of the fact that during the Civil War 267 men were executed by the military authorities. 141 were executed for desertion with Abe's approval. He was tougher on deserters than his counterpart, Jeff Davis.

PARDONS

However, little is said or known of Jeff Davis' compassion for those who received the same treatment in the Confederate Army. He was a kind and generous man and commuted nearly every death sentence for desertion that reached his desk.

"The poorest use of a soldier," he said, "was to shoot him." He kept this knowledge a secret.

Both men were criticized by the professional military for their leniency and disregard for military law and discipline.

DELIVER US FROM PROVERBS

D are we count the times we have been put off or have found our lives affected by the dictates of conventional wisdom as expressed by some proverbial cliche and enforced by someone of authority: a parent, a government official or a superior at work? We have all heard them: Spare the rod and spoil the child; I pulled myself up by my bootstraps; if it was good enough for me, it's good enough for you. Many have suffered!

Not so with Abe, who cared little for such wisdom and did not allow it to govern his life. Although he had only a "blab school education," his son would get an excellent, college education. When Robert failed all but one of the entrance exams to Harvard, he then was sent to Phillips Exeter Academy for a year to prepare for those exams. He passed them and graduated from Harvard. As usual, Abe's gospel applied reverse English to the proverbial bootstraps cliche. "I can't pull my son down by the bootstraps I pulled myself up with."

A STRICT JUDGE

Lincoln loved to tell of his experiences as a practicing attorney. One of his favorites was about Judge B who was so strict that he would hang a man for blowing his nose on the sidewalk but would quash the indictment if you didn't say which hand he blew it with in the indictment.

One day the judge presided over a murder trial, and the defendant was an old political ally. The jury came back with a verdict of guilty, and this put the judge in quite a "tissie". Would he be loyal to his principles of justice or to his old friend? After a lengthy period of thoughtful silence, the judge finally turned to the condemned and in the kindest way asked, "When would you like to get hung?"

THREE MEN IN A BED

In our history much has been made about the sleeping practices of our two most popular presidents, Washington and Lincoln. As a mark of distinction and pride, many east coast inns displayed the sign "George Washington Slept Here" to entice customers. If their claims were true, George would have been as old as Methuselah to have spent a night in every one of those beds. Comedians humoursly referred to this phenomena as the real reason why Washington was the Father of our Country.

Abe also slept around a lot. However in his instance, it has not been the number of beds or where he slept that has captured the interest and imagination of writers, but the length of the bed and who was in it. Nearly six feet four, his lenthy frame did not fit most beds. As a result, Abe's feet either extended over the foot board, or he was forced to sleep diagonally—tragically the position

he died in at the Peterson home, April 15, 1865.

In recent years there has been a spate of books and articles emphasizing that Abe slept with other men. In dwelling on this fact these writers intimate or strongly suggest that Lincoln had a special attraction for men. While this practice has been reported by historians, little was made of it. In Lincoln's day privacy came at a high price. The sleeping patterns of the period were dictated by the necessities of poverty and the scarcity of facilities. Thus, there was nothing strange or aberrant about men or women—even strangers— sleeping together. Lawyers slept three in a bed as they plied their trade on the old Eight Judicial Circuit in Illinois. While it would be most presumptuous to judge these writers' motives, their works tend to appeal to sensational and prurient interests or may be used to justify particular life styles.

GOOD FRIENDS CAN HAVE VICES!

Abe's friendships were based on personality and loyalty. Each relationship was a private matter with little regard for community standards of acceptable behavior. To Lincoln a friend was a friend through thick or thin.

Billy Herndon, his most enduring law partner, drank and was a free thinker. Mary Lincoln despised him. Didn't matter; he and Billy had an understanding. Ward Lamon was a big, rowdy man, who drank, got in fist fights and was frequently thrown in jail. Many a time Abe went Lamon's bail. He was a fellow lawyer and a loyal friend. Lamon went to Washington as Abe's bodyguard and Marshall of Washington. After Lincoln was re-elected in '64, rumors circulated that the President might be assassinated. That night, after Abe retired, Lamon, armed with handguns and knives, lay down in front of Lincoln's bedroom door until early dawn. Before the President arose Ward was gone, and Abe never knew about the incident.

When critics exposed his friends' bad behavior, Abe usually defended them and frequently dismissed it with, "Well, it's been my experience, that folks who have no vices have generally very few virtues."

SIPPING THROUGH THE BUNGHOLE

When Bill Greene, Abe's helper at Offutt's Store during his New Salem days, was tricked by a small time gambler, Lincoln became incensed at the slicker for taking advantage of his rather simple minded friend. Lincoln told Greene to bet the gambler the best fur hat in the store that he could lift a barrel of whiskey and take a drink from the bunghole. The gambler readily accepted the bet, and to his surprise, Abe did it.

PRESUME THE JUDGE KNOWS NOTHING

Abe was not a legal scholar. His second partner, Stephen Logan, was a highly respected and well trained lawyer who did much to help Abe become a good lawyer. In Logan's estimation, "I don't think he studied very much. I think he learned his law more in the study of cases....He got to be a pretty good lawyer though his general knowledge of law was never very formidable. But he would study out his case and make about as much of it as anybody."

His preparation of briefs on appeals cases was thorough, and he took nothing for granted. In them every precedent was researched to its origin, sometimes being traced back to the beginnings of English common law. Herndon asked him why his briefs were written that way, and Abe replied, "I dare not trust this case on presumptions that this court knows all things. I argued the case on the presumption that the court did not know any thing." As a result of these diligent methods, Abe was very successful before the Illinois Supreme Court, appearing in at least 300 cases.

BOOK LARNIN'S GOOD

Abe was a great respector of the knowledge and wisdom revealed by the written word contained in books. In his first address on "Discoveries and Inventions" he was convinced that the discovery of the written word was man's greatest invention. It liberated man from the bondage of the past and the local. There was nothing wrong with what has often been derisively called "book larnin", and he eloquently articulated the power of the printed word before a crowd of farmers, businessmen and scientists at the Wisconsin State Fair in 1859.

"A capacity, and taste, for reading, gives access to whatever has already been discovered by others. It is the key...to the already solved problems...and...it gives a relish, a facility, for successfully pursuing the yet unsolved ones."

ABE'S BUSTIN' OUT ALL UNDER

Besides being a great story teller, Abe did possess the faculty of humorous invention. Usually these occasions were a spontaneous reaction to an incident which befell him. Ward Lamon told of the time when Abe split the seam of his trousers while in court. Judge Davis and the crowd roared with laughter at Abe's unexpected revelation, and his fellow lawyers circulated a petition to raise the money to buy him a new pair. Abe's response to their good natured ribbing was, "I can contribute nothing to the end in view.

THE ONEIDEA COURT

At one time all of the justices on the Illinois Supreme Court were graduates of the Oneidea Law School.

Upon making this observation, Abe wryly commented that Illinois now had a One Idea court.*

This cartoon is based on a display that was once at the Old Capital in Springfield, Illinois.

READING WITH EARS; HEARING WITH EYES

When Abe was in Springfield, he usually arrived at the office about an hour after Billy Herndon, his third and most enduring partner, had opened it.

The first thing he did was pick up a newspaper, spread himself out on an old sofa and read aloud, much to Herndon's discomfort.

Billy frequently complained to Abe about his reading out loud, to which Abe replied, "I have to hear it and read it at the same time, else I'll forget it." This practice was a habit Lincoln acquired when he was in 'blab school' and one which he never outgrew.

HE MIGHT HAVE STAYED HOME

Throughout most of his adult life, Abe considered himself a homely man. Tall and skinny with a long neck and sharp facial features he felt himself unattractive to women.

Often his ungainly appearance was a subject of jokes Lincoln made while debating and making speeches. The crowds loved them, but Abe's humor eventually became a self-inflicted political liability. Although he might have been kidding, his image as a homely man spread back east. Major Republicans were most concerned and took steps to downplay his ugliness, even to the point of having bogus pictures painted showing him to be a handsome man.

The following story is the kind that he often told about himself: One day Abe was riding through the woods when he met a woman, also on horseback, who stopped and said:

"Well, for land sake, you are the homeliest man I ever saw."

"Yes, madam, but I can't help it," replied Abe.

"No, I supposed not," she observed, "but you might stay at home."

EQUALS IS EQUALS

As a young, Illinois legislator, Abe Lincoln proposed that white women be given the right to vote in the 1835-36 session of the state legislature. He was able to get a second on his resolution, which was somewhat of a miracle for its time. Needless to say, an all white, male legislature voted it down with only 2 votes for the ladies— Abe's and the man's who seconded the resolution.

Some recent historians have contended that Abe was not genuine with this resolution and that his action was a tongue in cheek joke. In those days, under Illinois law, women could not own property or pay taxes, thus they would have been disqualified had Lincoln's resolution passed. It is certainly true that women were little more than chattels under Common Law, but the author believes that old dog just won't hunt. This is especially true if we consider the numerous positive responses of women who met him, and the fact that the ladies possess an intuitive skill in assessing masculine put downs and patronizing men who rarely, if ever, comprehend. Trusting the recorded observations of the ladies, Abe's respect and treatment of women was genuine.

THE INNOCENT BONE OF CONTENTION

At times, Abe's wisdom and wit revealed ironic truths about the destinies of mankind. The following observation of what frequently happens to the weak when they become the object of a conflict between the mighty is brief and most profound.

THE SACRIFICIAL PRIZE

After an angry and dangerous contro-versy (fight) the parties made friends by dividing the bone of contention."

SPARED BY THE ABSENCE OF APPETITE

In an address to the temperance group, The Washingtonian Society, Abe Lincoln agreed with their methods for the care of alcoholics. It was non-sectarian and employed methods of persuasion and self improvement by getting persons to take pledges of abstinence. The Society believed that drunkenness was a vicious habit, and its victims should be treated as ill and not as criminals. He sympathized with their plight, questioning the pious attitudes of those not addicted to hard spirits.

"In my judgement," he stated, "such of us as have never fallen victims,(to alcohol) have been spared more from the absence of appetite, than from any mental or moral superiority over those who have."

MORE FACTS, LESS OPINION

Lincoln was hired as co-counsel in the famous Rock Island Bridge Case as an afterthought. A steamboat had crashed into the railroad bridge at Rock Island, Illinois, and the steamboat company was suing the bridge company for damages. The real objective of the steamboat people was to stop the competition of the railroads, which were eating into the river trade. Traditional law was on the side of the steamboat interests, and the judge and counsel for both sides tended to agree, with the exception of Lincoln. He visited the wreck's site, studied the location and the Mississippi's currents and, based on the flatboat experiences of his youth, concluded the wreck was the result of pilot error.

At the trial, the judge allowed Abe to present his findings but instructed the jury that their decisions must be based on the law and not the facts. Some of the jurors agreed with Abe's facts, resulting in a hung jury. A series of similar cases were initiated with railroad lawyers using Lincoln's defense and securing the same results. Lincoln had established a precedent of facts changing judicial opinion.

While visiting the site, supposedly, he talked with a teenage boy who was fishing near the bridge. "Son," he said, "I suppose you know all about this river."

"Sure, mister," the boy said. "It was here before I was born, and it's been here ever since."

"Well," responded Abe, "it's good to be out here where there is so much fact and so little opinion."

THE MOST WORDS INTO THE SMALLEST IDEAS

Although he probably never heard the popular cliche, "Keep it short and keep it simple," Abe practiced it. Lincoln's letters and speeches are masterpieces of brevity and usage of the precise word.

Lincoln detested long winded, wordy speakers and dropped many a humorous quip regarding them. He once described an exceptionally loquacious speaker: "He could compress the most words into the smallest ideas of any man I ever met."

EVERY BLADE A STUDY

Not only did Abe believe that everyone in a democracy needed an education, but it was alright for the government to help provide one. There was no occupation—even farming—that could not be improved from such endeavor.

Lincoln was intrigued by the new inventions and methods discovered by modern science. As President, he was constantly urging government officials and private enterprise to adopt new methods and tools. An educated body politic could invent and apply these scientific discoveries to industry and the efficient production of goods, thereby making the nation and its people richer, more prosperous and more secure.

To further the war effort, Abe directed General Herman Haupt, army engineering genius, to contact scientists for their suggestions on war related research. He made a serious effort to practice what he preached and is the only president who holds a patent from the United States government.

THE DUELING DUDES OF SPRINGFIELD

Probably the most embarrassing incident in Lincoln's life involved the proposed duel with the Illinois State Auditor, James Shields. What started out as humorous political satire almost ended in tragedy. It was caused by a series of anonymous articles appearing in the Whig newspaper, The Sangamo Journal, entitled, "Letters From Lost Township" by Aunt "Becca" (Rebecca). Abe wrote most of them with Mary and her friend, Julia Jayne, making some contributions. The major target of Aunt 'Becca's scorn was Democrat Shields.

Shields considered himself the darling of the ladies and the answer to every maiden's prayer. His attitude and appearance disgusted Mary, and she took personal delight in deflating his pretentious behavior. Through Aunt "Becca" she slashed him to the quick, comparing him to "a lock of cat fur which was floating about without heft of earthly substance above a cat fight."

Shields could take the political attack, but his ego would not accept the "cat fluff." He immediately commenced a series of actions from which neither man would back down and eventually resulted in Abe being challenged to a duel.

Before actual blows were exchanged, Abe regained his good sense. According to the code duello, since he was challenged, he could choose the weapons and dictate the terms of the duel.

Lincoln cleverly devised the conditions of combat whereby he would win, as revealed by the following directions:

"1st. Weapons-Cavalry broadswords of the largest size, precisely equal in all respects-and such as now used by the cavalry company at Jacksonville.

2nd. Position-A plank ten feet long, & from nine to twelve inches broad to be firmly fixed on edge, on the ground, as the line between us which neither is to pass his foot over upon forfeit of his life. Next a line drawn on the ground on either side of said plank & parallel with it, each at the distance of the whole length of the sword and three feet additional from the plank; and the passing of his own such line by either party during the fight shall be deemed a surrender of the contest."

Under these terms Shields could not touch Lincoln, while his opponent could chop him in half.

The combatants were at the dueling site on the Missouri side of the Mississippi River before Shields finally realized what could happen to him, and a compromise settlement was struck.

Lincoln learned a lot from that duel. Being a man of reason and thoroughly committed to solving conflict by the law, he found the incident was contrary to his foundational beliefs, and it embarrassed him. After that , he continued to attack his political enemies' politics but not their character.

GOT THREE, BOTH WANT TWO!

Once as Abe lugged his two howling, squirming sons, Tad and Willie, home, a neighbor asked, "Why, Mister Lincoln, what's the matter?"

Abe replied, "Just what's the matter with the whole world. I've got three walnuts, and each one of them wants two."

Although this lovable story is definitely Lincolnesque and plausible, it has not been authenticated.

DICTATING A NEW ADDRESS

Another of Abe's bad habits, as far as most persons were concerned, was that of talking to himself. He was constantly observed expressing his thoughts in this manner. It irritated many observers and caused them to question his mental capacities.

Regardless of their evaluations and judgments of this behavior, it was the method that he devised for composing his speeches, letters and position papers. It, like reading aloud to himself, was also a by-product of blab schools. If this habit were a detriment to him, how much more would he have accomplished without it? Can you imagine a world with greater speeches than the Gettysburg and Second Inaugural Addresses? Contrarily, had he conformed to the accepted behavior of society and, by doing so, never written those beautiful lines, what an empty world it would be without them!

JOKES BY TOM

Tom Lincoln was a convivial fellow, fond of good company and a leader of grocery store dialogue. His chief earthly pleasure was cracking jokes and telling stories to chums who gave their laughter and applause.

Although the two men were never close, the father's art passed on to the son and was one of the principal sources of Abe's humor. Lincoln presented many a story with, "As my old father, Tom Lincoln, used to say, 'There are many more ways of kill'n a cat than choking it to death with dry bread.'" As usual, there was a profound truth contained within a story or statement.

THE IGNORANT AND VICIOUS SHALL SHARE

The Republican Party that Abe Lincoln led to power in 1861, earnestly believed in the supremacy of the national government to advance the freedom and equality of all citizens. Furthermore, the Constitution forged by the Founding Fathers created the federal government as the instrument for realizing the promises of the Declaration of Independence: life, liberty and the pursuit of happiness.

Abe cherished those inalienable rights propounded by Tom Jefferson, and every citizen was entitled to receive them. This aspect of his philosophy was eloquently expressed in this fragment written about 1854:

"Most governments have been based on the denial of the equal rights of man; ours began by affirming those rights. They said, some men are too ignorant and vicious to share in government. Possibly so, said we; and, by your system, you would always keep them ignorant and vicious."

THE SKINNIEST HORSE

Many of the stories about Abe Lincoln are the products of his unique way of looking at problems or situations and his reaction to them. He was not a slave to the dictates of conventional wisdom. This mind set and outlook contributed to Abe's greatness as President.

One time Abe bet a judge that he could find a skinnier horse than His Honor. The judge accepted the bet and set out to find the poorest, skinniest plug horse in the area. On the day of the contest, the jurist proudly displayed his walking bone heap, only to be beat out by Abe who displayed a local carpenter's saw horse. The judge protested Abe's entry but had to concede that he had been euchred, paid off the bet and laughed about it for years.

A THOUGHT AT A TIME AND SHUFFLING A LINE

Writing came hard to Abe. Early in life he established his practical method of composition. Whenever he had a beautiful thought about a particular issue or abstraction, he jotted it down on a bit of paper or envelope and stuffed it into his hat or pockets.

When he had the time, usually at night since he suffered from insomnia from the days of his youth, he would place those statements on a table or any other available furniture. Then he sorted those pieces of paper into piles according to the issues involved. After that, he would shuffle and re-arrange the small pieces of paper until they became sentences, paragraphs and themes. When they stated precisely what he wished to say about a particular subject, he wrote them and, falling back on his blab school education, frequently committed them to memory. They became a reservoir of quotes for his writings and speeches.

Lincoln, 206.

NEVER OLD ENOUGH

A t this time Charlie B is not old enough
either.

HE ARGUED HIS OPPONENT'S CASE AND WON

When a young lawyer who opposed him in a case before the Illinois Supreme Court lacked the funds to stay a week until the appeal was heard, Abe volunteered to argue both sides before that judicial body. In the following letter Lincoln informed his absent adversary of the judges' decision:

My Dear Mr. Bishop,
The Supreme Court came in on the appointed day and I did my best to keep faith with you. Apparently I argued your case better than my own, for the court has just sent down a rescript in your favor. Accept my heartiest congratulations.
A. Lincoln

CRUEL AND UNUSUAL PUNISHMENT

One day rotund, jovial Judge David Davis absentmindedly sentenced a young thief to seven years in the legislature. Ward Lamon quickly whispered in Davis' ear, "You mean prison don't you?"

The judge, whose informality was equalled only by his sense of justice, quickly corrected himself. He was one of Abe's best friends and campaign manager at Chicago in 1860, which secured Lincoln the Republican nomination. He was Lincoln's lawyer, and during his presidency, Abe appointed him to the U.S. Supreme Court.

THE WORST FIEND

If lawyers followed Abe's recommended behavior, their image with the public would be much higher. Also, the public itself would be less litigious and perhaps inclined to resolve problems amicably.

Abe counseled, "Never stir up litigation. A worse man can scarcely be found than one who does this. Who can be more nearly a fiend than he who habitually overhauls the register of deeds in search of defects in titles, whereon to stir up strife, and put money in his pocket? A moral tone ought to be infused into the profession which should drive such men out of it."

WRITING JUST RIGHT

In all of Abe's endeavors, diligence was his by-word. Do a task as soon as possible and do it right. When he accepted an invitation to give an important speech, he immediately started, working on it until tired of the project before putting it aside. Whenever he had spare time or had a new idea regarding the project, he picked it up and reworked it. His partner, William Herndon, observed that he was a thoughtful, careful writer who spent hours sorting out his points and tightening his logic and phrasing. A speech was never finished until the moment he gave it.

Being an astute politician, whenever he delivered an important speech, he read his script and rarely made extemporaneous remarks, realizing their danger.

ABE'S WHATYOUCALLIT

Abe Lincoln is the only President of the United States to hold a patent. A result of a frontier skill acquired from handling flatboats on the Ohio and Mississippi river systems, he was well acquainted with boats being grounded on sand-bars. Based on flotation principles it probably would have worked, but Lincoln never tested the device under real conditions and put it aside.

THE LONG AND THE SHORT OF IT

Mary Lincoln never posed for photographs with her husband standing. Abe frequently described them as the "long and the short of it" and said that she almost came up to his short ribs. She detested such comparisons as hickish and did her best to get him to stop.

At times in her presence he would play the country hick, much to her chagrin, and teasingly accuse her of trying to make of him a silk purse out of a sow's ear. His pet name for her was Molly, and she always called him Mr. Lincoln. On the photos she won but not on his flights of country behavior. Thus Abe was always seated when their pictures were made.

BECOME A SLAVE AND TAKE THE GOOD OF IT

Throughout Lincoln's life he wrote many passages denoting his contempt for the institution of slavery. He accepted the Founding Fathers' position that slavery was a necessary evil which had to be tolerated in order to establish our country, especially since they held out the hope of the institution's gradual eradication. Morally it was wrong, and when the opinion spread that slavery was morally right, he opposed it.

Abe was also a master at logically attacking the positions and arguments of individuals based upon personal interest and greed rather than the truth and humane public policy. When pro slave advocates George Fitzhugh and Senator James Hammond argued that slavery was a wonderful institution and that the bondsmen were happy and content with their lives in the South, Abe countered with, "Although volume upon volume has been written to prove slavery a very good thing, we never hear of the man who wishes to take the good of it by being a slave himself."

Lang, 36; Oates, 137, 152; Jaffa, 202.

IS A CHESTNUT HORSE A HORSE CHESTNUT?

In their famous debates, Douglas constantly accused the Republicans and Lincoln of advocating full social and racial equality for the blacks. His biggest scarecrow was the charge that the Republicans favored interracial marriage. Over and over again he asked, "Do you want your daughter to marry a N_____?" He knew that most whites abhorred such a practice and would vote against any candidate that made the slightest suggestion of such a policy.

Lincoln knew what Douglas was attempting to do and understood the fears of the whites. To allay those fears he was forced to agree with Douglas that the blacks were not equal to whites in all respects. However, he insisted, the Negro was entitled to all those rights contained in the Declaration of Independence: life, liberty and the pursuit of happiness.

Furthermore, Lincoln continued, Douglas was twisting his words with "a specious and fantastic arrangement of words, by which a man can prove a horse chestnut to be a chestnut horse."

NO GRIEVANCE JUSTIFIES MOB LAW

It was during his New Salem days that Lincoln's talent for writing commenced. He considered many topics, but his favorite and most enduring subject was politics. Often, under a pseudonym, he blasted the Democrats with partisan humor and sarcasm.

However, when not in the heat of partisan battle, he produced wonderful essays and speeches. During 1838, his prose varied from the sublime to the ridiculous. In January he delivered his Young Men's Lyceum Speech entitled, "The Perpetuation Of Our Political Institutions." This speech was a great defence for law and order and expressed a sincere fear that mob violence could destroy this country. It also provoked a modern school of literary criticism and psychology on Lincoln. Later that year under the name of John Bubberhead, he published partisan polemics ridiculing Douglas and the Democrats.

To the best of my knowledge, John Bubberhead has never been quoted, but who can forget, "There is no grievance that is a fit object of redress by mob law," written by a self-educated twenty-nine year old man.

Oates, 53; Living Lincoln, 20-27.

A BAD SPLIT INSTEAD OF A STRIKE

When Abe first arrived as the only Whig Congressman from Illinois in the Thirtieth Congress, he, Mary, and their two oldest sons stayed at Mrs. Ann Sprigg's boarding house. He was short on cash, and in order to get by until his first check from the Congress, he borrowed money from his old political nemesis but good friend, Steve Douglas, who was already a power in the Senate.

At first, Mary and Abe enjoyed Washington, but in time Molly grew tired of being cooped up in their one room and taking meals with the rest of the boarders. She and the boys reluctantly went to Lexington, Kentucky, to stay with her father while Abe finished his term. He missed his family and to relieve his loneliness learned to bowl and studied Euclid to the sixth book. Although an awkward bowler and comical to watch, he played the game with zest and had a lot of fun with other players.

His poor game on the lanes did not hurt him, but he had some bad splits as a politician. The Whig Party was slowly falling apart. It opposed the Mexican War and was against acquiring territory, especially if it were to be used to expand slavery. As a loyal Whig, Abe voted with them, angering his constituents in Illinois, where the war and Manifest Destiny were very popular. Come 1848, Abe realized that he was not electable and did not seek re-election.

OUT, OUT DAMNED SPOT(ty) LINCOLN

Abe Lincoln's term as a Whig in the 30th Congress proved to be a disappointment to him and the folks back home. Out of that experience he acquired the uncomplimentary nickname of "Spotty Lincoln" from the Democrats.

The Whigs considered the war an outright act to seize territory for the expansion of slavery, and not as Steve Douglas and the Democrats and southerners maintained that we were filling out our country to its natural boundaries or our Manifest Des-tiny. Furthermore, they accused Polk of deliberately provoking the incident that led to the declaration of war on Mexico and of lying about the spot of land where our countrymen had shed their blood. As the spokesman for the Whigs, Abe presented his Spot Resolutions demanding that Polk show the spot of sacred soil where Americans' blood had been shed, implying that the President was lying. Polk ignored the new up-start from Illinois, knowing that the war was popular in most of the country.

While Abe's position was basically true and endeared him to the Mexican people, it went over like a lead balloon in Illinois and was a factor in his not seeking re-election in 1848. Morally and factually Abe was right, and the event left a bitter taste causing him to temporarily get out of politics. However, in or out of politics, Illinois Democrats never let him forget "Spotty Lincoln."

KEEPING IT SIMPLE

Lincoln was a very effective trial lawyer and was especially good with juries. As a surveyor and lawyer for many years, he was known by most of the jurors in the Eighth Judicial Circuit. His remarkable memory enabled him to identify by name, residence and family nearly every juror in the area.

In the courtroom, Abe maintained that personal connection, appearing to speak to every juror. His summations were interspersed with folksy anecdotes and few technical terms. As he warned Herndon, "Billy, don't shoot too high, aim lower and the common people will understand you. They are the ones you want to reach."

Lincoln, 98; Peterson, 339.

LET 'EM TEAR THE HOUSE DOWN!

According to many of today's critics on parenting, the Lincolns would be considered permissive parents, especially Abe!! On Sundays, when Molly attended church, he took Willie and Tad to the law office, much to Billy Herndon's distress. Abe never paid any attention to the children's destructive acts and allowed them to do whatever they wished. Billy considered them wild Banshees who left the place looking like it had been hit by a tornado.

Many of Lincoln's friends suggested to him that the boys needed some good, old fashioned discipline, but he turned thumbs down on their advice with this hearsay rebuttal: "My Father ruled me with an iron discipline, and I didn't like it, and my little codgers are going to love me even if I have to let them tear the house down." So Abe never spanked them, although Mrs. Lincoln occasionally did get to the "seat" of the problem.

Although the Lincolns failed to observe the popular adage espoused by the proponents of "Spare the rod and spoil the child," their only son to reach adulthood was very successful. Robert Todd Lincoln was in President Garfield's Cabinet and was United States' Ambassador to Great Britain under Mckinley. He also did well as a business man, becoming President of the Pullman Corporation. Could Dr. Spock have modelled his advice for child rearing on the Lincolns?

SPECIAL ABILITY FOR A WINNING POLITICAN

Abe was a skillful politician who had faith in the good ones to make democracy work. Properly motivated men in private or public life do make valuable contributions to the orderly function and harmony of society.

While there is a tendency for those in the private sector to look down on politicians, government business is no better or worse than private, for politics is but a mirror of the vested interests that elects them. In all avenues of human endeavor scoundrels, incompetents and irrational zealots do secure admission. This type of practitioner was frequently the target of Abe's best sarcastic barbs. When asked what was the most valuable special ability for a winning politician, he replied, "To be able to raise a cause which will produce an effect, and then fight the effect." Think about it.

A SUPERIOR OPPORTUNITY TO DO GOOD

Abe had great faith in the legal profession as peace makers and insurers of societal tranquility. Much of a lawyer's work, in his estimation, was keeping people out of court. "Discourage litigation," he counselled attorneys. "Persuade your neighbors to compromise whenever you can. Point out to them how the nominal winner is often a real loser—in fees, expenses, and waste of time. As a peacemaker the lawyer has a superior opportunity of being a good man. There will still be business enough."

OLD ABE IS PUTTIN' ON (H)AIRS

Abe Lincoln was the first president to wear a beard. No one knows why he decided to sprout one. During the presidential campaign of 1860, certain "True Republicans" from New York State had worried that Lincoln's homely looks might cost their party votes and had suggested that he grow a beard and wear standing collars—the former to improve his unflattering face and the latter to shorten his long neck. Was it to cover up this ugliness? He laughingly said so many times. Was it in response to a letter from little eleven year old Grace Bedell from Westfield, New York? Maybe? He did stop at Westfield on his way to Washington, DC in February of '61, and spoke with her—even kissed her! Maybe he was just bored; or like Thoreau, he did it because he wanted to! Who cares?

After growing facial hair he was criticized for doing so, and cartoonists pictured him puttin' on (h)airs. One thing is certain. His experiment set the style for all of the remaining 19th century presidents.

Presently, the bulk of mankind has a strong affection for him and admires his looks. He is described as statuesque, dignified, Lincolnesque. OK! Like the old saying goes, "Beauty is in the eye of the beholder." But in his day, it meant homely as all get out.

Lincoln, 258; Lang, 87; Oates, 59.

CAESAR'S HAIR

Abe certainly would be luke warm to modern testing methods, polygraphs, psychological batteries, IQ tests, etc. In the selection of a person for a job, long time friend, Jesse Weik said of Lincoln, "He believed there were other if not better ways of determining a man's fitness for a given task or position than the regulation test questions."

One time Lincoln had a problem with the War Department regarding the appointment of a colonel of a black regiment and wrote the following note to an Army Officer Review Board:

"I personally wish Jacob Freese, of New Jersey, to be appointed colonel for a colored regiment, and this regardless of whether he can tell the exact shade of Julius Caesar's hair."

WHENCE COME CAPITAL

Lincoln was a strong believer in the labor theory of wealth, and in his first State of The Union Address to the Congress in December of 1861, he made the following statement:

"Labor is prior to, and independent of, capital. Capital is only the fruit of labor, and could never have existed if labor had not first existed. Labor is the superior of capital, and deserves much the higher consideration. Capital has its rights, which are as worthy of protection as any other rights."

WHAT TO DO WITH THAT HAT?

Without Abe Lincoln's stove pipe hat, the history books would be a little thinner. That hat has been a source of conversation and anecdote ever since the Rail Splitter moved into the White House. It has had a personality and function of its own. Abe's chapeau has rescued many a desperate speaker, politician and minister from the throes of a dying audience. It has had more roles than the facets on the bogus diamond ring Uncle Fred got for Aunt Millie. While most politicians have had to wear many hats to survive, Lincoln's sombrero had such a broad brim that he could get by with one.

Besides protecting him from the weather, the stove pipe served as a brief case, a secretary for the storage of his correspondence, a moving van and a repository of his notes. Drop the van and the preceding statement is relatively true. Yes, the portly lady did sit on his hat, and after viewing her bountiful posterior, he did remark to the effect that he knew it would not fit. Did Steve Douglas hold Abe's hat when he took the oath of office as President in '61? Since the sources of that story are the product of unverified reminiscence, most historians have concluded that it is just too good to be true. Yet, Donald includes the vignette in his recent book, *Lincoln*. Maybe, like the portly lady's derriere, the larger truth redeems any falsity of de' tail.

IN LIKE PHARAOH

Old Abe has worn many hats, and one of the most consistent and enduring to the nation and the world is the image of the Great Emancipator. Almost unanimously to the blacks of his day, he was their savior, and they were among the first to propose raising a monument to his memory.

OUT LIKE MOSES

Frederick Douglass cared for Lincoln and considered him a friend, but he was one of the few blacks of that era who had mixed feelings about the President. Qualifying his position, he wrote, "Old Abe came in like pharaoh...(and) went out like Moses."

NEVER SELL OUT OLD FRIENDS

In the senatorial election of 1858, many eastern Republicans, including Horace Greeley, were content with Steve Douglas' record and proposed allowing him to run unopposed in Illinois. This infuriated the Sucker State Republicans who were especially chagrined at the eastern establishment meddling in their politics. Heeding Abe Lincoln's advice, "Never sell out old friends to buy old enemies," they chose the Rail Splitter and gave Douglas the race of his life.

Abe lost the election, although he received more popular votes. Douglas was re-elected due to gerrymandering of the Illinois State Legislature by the Democrats following the 1850 census. In those days United States Senators were elected by the state legislatures and not by the voters. The famous Lincoln-Douglas Debates accomplished two objectives: The debates derailed Douglas from his well positioned drive toward the White House and propelled Abe into it in 1861.

CROSSING FOX RIVER

Between November of '60, when Lincoln was elected and before he was inaugurated in March '61, some of the southern slave states seceded from the Union. Editors and other influential persons pressured Lincoln to divulge his plans for keeping the country together when he became President. Since he could do nothing during the interim, he prudently told them nothing and responded with this fable:

Many years ago a group of lawyers were riding the judicial circuit in Illinois. A rain storm came up flooding the area and making Fox River impassable. Their progress blocked, the lawyers settled down for the night at a nearby tavern. In their conversations after supper they all expressed concern about the flooded river and how they would get across it the next day.

With the group that evening was the Presiding Elder of the Methodist Church, who knew the country well and had crossed the river many times. He was asked what he was going to do about fording the stream the next day, and the Elder replied, "Gentlemen, I've crossed Fox River when it was high and when it was low, when it was covered with ice and when it was muddy, and when its current was fast and when it was slow. I have crossed it many times and understand it well, but I have one fixed rule with regard to that river. I never cross Fox River 'till I get to it."

DOES YOUR HEAD KNOW WHEN YOUR FEET GET COLD?

Abe was often asked if he wrote his own jokes, to which he replied that they were the product of far better story tellers than he. He was not a wholesaler but a "re-teller" of stories. When something happened that tickled his funny bone, his compulsive disposition to blurt out a spontaneous quip or joke just happened. It was hard for him to suppress this compulsive behavior, and his one liners frequently got him into trouble.

One day while reviewing troops he came upon a soldier at least six feet nine. Sizing up the tall stranger, he impishly looked up into the soldier's face and asked, "Say, soldier, does your head know when your feet get cold?"

Of course the ranks exploded, and, as usual, the President had again temporarily shattered army discipline.

SURPRISE SURPRISE

ew people are aware of the mass of quality written material Abe produced, much of it before he became President. His out-put far exceeds that of any of his three favorite authors or works. Including his printed speeches, Lincoln wrote 50,000 more words than Shakespeare, 150,000 more words than are contained in the *Bible* including the *Apocrypha*, and Burns isn't in the running. To the million plus words of his writings must be added additional millions of quoted verbal statements.

Some scholars have argued that if Abe had never been elected President, he would still be recognized as a great writer. Possibly so. However, it was the Presidency that gave him a pulpit to the world's audience and his masterful handling of that position which ignited the enduring interest in his words.

LAMON, SING ME A SAD, SWEET SONG

I WANDERED TO THE VILLAGE, TOM, I SAT BENEATH THE TREE; UPON THE SCHOOLYARD PLAYING GROUND WHICH SHELTER'D YOU AND ME. BUT NONE WERE THERE TO GREET ME TOM; AND FEW WERE LEFT TO KNOW, THAT PLAYED WITH US UPON THE GRASS, SOME TWENTY YEARS AGO..!*

LAMON

COURT IN SESSION

* 'TWENTY YEARS AGO' by WM. WILLING

The stressful demands of leading our country during the Civil War deeply burdened Abe Lincoln, but his tremendous inner strength and resilience enabled him to withstand the greatest challenge any president ever faced. And yet he could be very sentimental and frequently shed tears in public-—an activity which real he-men are never supposed to do.

One of his dearest friends was Ward Hill Lamon. Abe brought him to Washington in '61, and appointed him marshal of the nation's capitol. Ward frequently served as the President's body guard and was most protective and loyal to his old friend. Though Laman was a big bruiser of a man who drank and frequently got into fights, Lincoln loved the way he played the banjo and sang songs. Some were bawdy, others were Negro nonsense songs, and some were downright tearjerkers. Often, throughout the years of their friendship, Abe for no apparent reason would ask, "Lamon. Play me one of your sad, sweet songs." Inevitably, Lincoln would shed tears as the big burly man played and sang such a tear jerker as William Willing's "Twenty Years Ago."

HONESTLY, ABE?

When asked if he ever told lies, Abe laughingly replied, "I hain't been caught lyin' yet, and I don't mean to be." Like all presidents, he was privy to confidential information which, if revealed, could have been extremely harmful to the nation. Therefore, in a more serious vein, he responded that he didn't deliberately lie but occasionally he did "Take economies with the truth."

This practice often irritated the press, Congress and important members in his administration. But at a timely moment when the whole truth did emerge, most respected his reasons for taking those economies.

Garry Wills, 187; Oates, 266.

ABE ON SLAVERY

I DON'T WANT HER AS A SLAVE!

Lincoln's natural tendency to sympathize with the slaves was strengthened by his own personal experiences with Negroes. William Fleurville was a good friend and his barber in Springfield. Abe did Billy's law work. When he boarded the train for Washington in early '61, the only person he selected to accompany him was black bodyguard, William Johnson. Abe wanted to give Johnson a job on the White House staff but could not because of the opposition of incumbent Negro servants.

He did not get excited over such matters as social equality and intermarriage, which Lincoln regarded as emotionally toned false issues. Throughout the last years of their political wars, Stephen Douglas repeatedly charged that Lincoln and the Republicans were for interracial marriage. The old shock question that put terror in the hearts of whites was continually raised, "Do you want your daughter to marry a _____?" Abe responded, "Now I protest against that counterfeit logic which concludes that, because I do not want a black woman for a slave I must necessarily want her for a wife. I need not have her for either. I can just leave her alone."

Of course there is the flip side of the question which few whites ever considered, but Abe did. Revealing a mixture of personal values and humor on the subject of interracial marriage, he wrote to David Locke in 1859, "I shall never marry a Negress, but I have no objection to anyone else doing so. If a White man wants to marry a Negro woman, let him if the Negro can stand it."

RACE AND MARRIAGE

ABE SIGNS A DECLARATION JULY FOURTH

The temperance movement commenced during the 1820's and continued to grow in influence throughout Lincoln's life. One of its largest elements was the Washingtonian Society. One of Abe's greatest speeches was presented to the Society in Springfield on February 22, 1842. In that speech, among many other points, he especially appreciated their contention that those addicted to drink were not unpardonable sinners forever damned to outer darkness and continued:

"As in Christianity, it is taught, so in this they teach, that
  'While the lamp holds out to burn,
  The vilest sinner may return.' "

Consistent with his beliefs in temperance and tolerance, Abe signed the Presidential Temperance Document on July 4. 1861. The Document was first circulated in 1833, and had been signed by ten previous presidents. Reputedly, President Harrison died before he could sign the certificate.

FOR THE MAN OR THE MONEY

The Republican Men's Club of Boston wanted Lincoln to address them at a Jefferson Day Dinner in 1859. He declined their invitation but wrote them a letter presenting his views as a Republican. In the letter he presented the basic principles of their party and contrasted them to those of current Democrats, specifically how the party of Jefferson (Democrats) had abandoned his principles, and the Republicans had adopted them. In particular, he stressed how Jefferson was devoted to preserving the personal rights of men, holding that property rights were secondary and inferior to personal rights.

Furthermore, he wrote, "The Democrats of today hold the liberty of one man to be absolutely nothing when in conflict with another man's right of property. Republicans, on the contrary, are for both the man and the dollar; but in cases of conflict, the man before the dollar."

TOM WROTE; ABE ACTED!

Abe Lincoln firmly believed and continually stated, "I have never had a feeling politically that did not spring from the sentiments embodied by the Declaration of Independence." "The new birth of freedom" Abe spoke of at Gettysburg referred to the emancipation of the slaves.

Thomas Jefferson, the principal author of the Declaration, genuinely believed that all men were created equal and believed that slavery was morally wrong and an evil that should be done away with. However, he frequently stated that he did not know what to do about it, and, as President, he did nothing toward eradicating the institution.

Like Jefferson in 1776, Abe was committed to the proposition that all men were created equal, but unlike the third president, who felt hopeless in dealing with the issue of slavery, Lincoln did something about it. He did away with it.

THE FLO' THROUGH THE GRAPEVINE

During the Civil War, every possible means was utilized by southern owners to isolate and keep information from their slaves. However, their chattels knew something of the existing state of affairs at every stage of the war. They were informed by what was termed the "grapevine telegraph."

From almost the beginning, the "grapevine" reported that Abe Lincoln and the Union were their route to freedom, and, whenever possible, they willingly helped the yankees. The slaves provided the North with an elaborate and effective intelligence system to a level which the Confederates never attained. Union generals soon learned that the information given by contraband slaves was true and of great value. That old slave "grapevine" was a conduit of information and intelligence helping Abe to save the Union and achieve their freedom.

Quarles, 46-53, 79, 267-272.

FRIEND DOUGLASS HITS A DOUBLE

At the reception following Lincoln's second inauguration, Abe stood in line shaking hands with hundreds of well wishers. Somebody informed him that Frederick Douglass was at the front door. The police wouldn't let him in, because he was a Negro.

Lincoln had him shown in at once and greeted him as his good friend, Douglass, shaking his hand and introducing him to the audience. The President also asked him what he thought of his Second Inaugural Address, to which Douglass replied he thought it a sacred effort. Thus, it was the first inaugural reception in the history of the Republic in which an American President had greeted a free black man and solicited his opinion.

A DIFFERENCE BETWEEN BEING PAID TO EAT AND PAYING FOR IT

To the person born in poverty who has had to fight and claw his way up to success, there often remains a contempt for those individuals who have had everything given to them without the shedding of one drop of sweat or expending a single calorie of energy. The self made man finds it hard not to resent, as the old saying goes, "Those who were born with a silver spoon in the mouth."

Abe was not a vindictive man, and he always bent over backwards trying not to be prejudiced against any individual because of his membership in some particular group, association, race, economic condition or denomination. And yet, beneath his reasoned outlook and polish, the harsh realities of his long struggle to pull himself up were occasionally expressed. While there is a lot of truth and humor in Abe's clever statement, "There is a difference in being paid to eat and paying for it," it is also tinged with the bitter irony known only to the poor.

DIFFERENT STRIKES

After Lincoln's successful Cooper Union Address in early 1860, repeat performances of the speech were well received throughout the Northeast, making him a more prominent, national political figure. No longer was he the country lawyer who slew the Little Giant in the Great Debates of '58. People wanted to see him and know his position on the vital issues facing the nation.

When asked about a shoe makers' strike at Lynn, Massachusetts, he said;

"Thank God we have a system of labor where there can be a strike. I do not know much about the matter...I am glad to see that a system of labor prevails in New England under which laborers can strike when they want to, where they are not obliged to work under all circumstances, and not tied down and obliged to labor whether you pay them or not! I like the system which lets a man quit when he wants to, and wish it might prevail everywhere...."

THE UGLY DUCKLING

During the 1860 presidential campaign a great demand came from the public for information and pictures of the Republican candidate, Abe Lincoln. So many of the easterners had heard tales about his ugliness that party stalwarts feared his appearance would cost votes. To combat this issue, Judge John M. Read of Pennsylvania commissioned John Henry Brown to paint a miniature that would be good looking regardless of "whether the original would justify it or not."

Can you imagine Abe Lincoln as Prince Charming? And we thought chopped pictures and doctored images were creatures of this century?

THE HONOR OF THE THING

After Lincoln had been President for a while, an old Springfield friend asked him, "How does it feel to be President of the United States?"

"You have heard of the man that had been tarred and feathered and was being ridden out of town on a rail? A man in the crowd asked him how he liked it, and his reply was that if it wasn't for the honor of the thing, he would just as soon get off and walk."

STAND WITH A MAN WHEN HE'S RIGHT

At times, due to partisan positions or the prevailing attitudes and biases of the voters, Abe was compelled to make "compromises with prejudice." He disliked doing so but could not find any other way to be a successful politician. However, he told trusted friends he loathed taking such positions and said that he looked forward to the day when he could always, "Stand with a man when he is right and against him when he is wrong. Stand with the abolitionist when he opposes the Kansas-Nebraska Act and against him when he advocates breaking the Fugitive Slave Law."

CAREFUL PLEADING

The writings of Lincoln are filled with hundreds of wise, profound quotes, brief and to the point. What a wonderful world it would be, how much happier we would all be and how many forests it would save from pulp paper mills if the legal profession would only follow this advice: "In the law I have found it good practice never to plead what you need not least you be obliged to prove what you cannot."

NOT CAREFUL ENOUGH

If today's judges demanded such brevity as suggested by Old Abe, we might not have less litigation, but certainly we would have swifter and better justice. His Honor would at least have the time to thoroughly read through all of that paper. Without a doubt, the cost to the taxpayers and the clients of the justice system would plummet.

AN OPEN WALLET POLICY

Another insight into the loving relationship that existed between Abe and Mary Lincoln was that regarding money. In the Lincolns' day the man made the money and controlled it. In many instances he doled out specific amounts of cash to his wife to manage the home and care for the family. Usually, this also called for an accounting. Under Common Law a woman might own wealth but could not control it.

During their marriage, Abe was quite modern for his time. If Mary needed money, she freely opened his wallet and took what she wanted. While other women begged, scrounged and did without, Mary shared her husband's wealth. Abe wasn't a greedy or possessive man regarding money. It was theirs.

THE CHEAPEST LAWYER

To Lincoln the law and its administration was an indispensable function of government which preserved peace and harmony for society. Because of this, everyone should have access to it. If a man could not afford justice, the profession was responsible for seeing that he got it. Fees should be reasonable, even for those who could afford them.

One time a Chicago firm had an important case valued at $2,500.00. It asked Springfield banker, John Bunn, to retain a good lawyer to represent them. He gave the case to his good friend, Lincoln. Abe won the case and sent the firm the $2,500.00 and a bill for $25.00.

Shortly thereafter, Bunn received the following letter from the Chicago firm "We asked you to hire the best lawyer in Springfield. Apparently, you got the cheapest."

Today's attorneys would certainly accommodate such a firm, making sure to give them the respect they yearn for.

BILLY'S LAST HAIRCUT FOR ABE

One of the first persons Abe came to know in Springfield was Billy Fleurville, a free black man from Haiti. Abe had first met Billy when the penniless young barber stopped at New Salem in route to Springfield in the fall of 1831. Abe took Billy to the Rutledge Tavern and informed the men that his new acquaintance needed work. From that meeting, Flourville made enough money to get to Springfield where he opened its first barber shop.

Billy the Barber's shop became the informal young men's social club at the state capitol and Abe's second home before his marriage in 1842. According to the locals, Billy had the sharpest wit and razor in town, and Lincoln gave him credit as the source of some of his best stories. The pair became close friends. Billy shaved and cut Lincoln's hair, and Abe did Billy's law work. Flourville styled the sixteenth President's beard. One of the most sorrowful leave-takings of the Rail Splitter was at the old barbershop where Billy cut Abe's hair for the last and final time.

Secretary of War, Edwin Stanton, was an autograph collector. One day Abe found a signature of John Quincy Adams on a piece of misplaced correspondence in his office. Knowing of Stanton's interest, he wrote a brief comment on it and sent the autograph to the Secretary of War. Little did Lincoln suspect that someday his own signature would be of far greater value. Ed got two for one.

THE SIX AND A HALF CENT OVERCHARGE

L incoln's honesty has been the source of many stories about good behavior, especially in children's books. However, there were authors who wanted Lincoln to be bigger than he actually was, and in their enthusiasm, they were a bit dishonest in their reportage of Abe's honesty. In 1883, Horatio Alger's book, *Abraham Lincoln, the Backwoods Boy,* had Abe walking miles to return six and a half cents to a lady he had overcharged at the Offut Store. Nice as it sounds, it just isn't so. Honestly!

Honesty is an admired character trait, and certainly Abe was a very honest man, as his peers knew. Among the lawyers, judges and people who worked with him in the Eighth Judicial Circuit, he had the reputation for being the most honest of the profession, but he never made that walk.

JUDGE DAVIS' CAPER AT THE WIGWAM

Abe's friend, lawyer, and campaign manager, Judge David Davis, was a dominate force at the Republican convention in Chicago in 1860. Lincoln was well known and liked by many of the delegates but was not a leading candidate. With political acumen and a bit of skullduggery he euchred the eastern Republicans out of their shorts and secured the nomination for Lincoln. In those days candidates did not appear at the convention. They were preoccupied with lofty and arcane matters while their lieutenants battled in the trenches and made deals. True to form, Abe stayed in Springfield but got wind of Davis' wheeling and dealing and was concerned. He sent the judge the following telegram: "Make no deals in my name." When informed of Abe's message, Davis's responded to his fellow Illinois Republicans, "Lincoln ain't here, and we is!" and continued brokering deals. And "is" they were. Between the counterfeit delegate passes allowing loyal Illinois Republicans to occupy the seats of the legitimate holders and stampede the convention and the goodies Davis passed out, Lincoln received the nomination. In this way, Davis picked much of Abe's cabinet and made Lincoln history.

WAS ABE A RACIST?

In a democracy a candidate must heed the wishes of his constituents, or he isn't elected. Regardless of his ideals and motives, "If he can't get elected, he can't do anything." This explains why some politicians originally secured office by conceding to their constituency's bigotry, and later in their careers reversing themselves.

Lincoln's statements regarding the superiority of the white race fit this category. During their famous debates Douglas, knowing the prejudices of the white male voters of Illinois, forced Lincoln into publicly making those statements. For Abe to have done otherwise was political suicide.

Although Abe felt compelled to make those racist remarks, at considerable political risk he always qualified his position with a moral justification for black rights. The following is a good example:"...Certainly the Negro is not our equal in color-—perhaps not in many other respects; still, in the right to put into his mouth the bread that his own hands have earned, he is the equal of every other man white or black. In pointing out that more has been given you, you cannot be justified in taking away the little which has been given him. All I ask for the Negro is that if you do not like him, let him alone. If God gave him but little, that little let him enjoy."

CAN YOU SPELL, MR. PRESIDENTS?

Little is known of the fact that both George Washington and Abe Lincoln had problems when it came to spelling. It is rumoured that Thomas Jefferson suffered from the same difficulty and stated that it was a very dull mind that could only spell a word one way. Lincoln struggled with spelling all of his life, and not long before his death he confessed to his long time friend, Judge David Davis, that he had finally learned how to spell "maintenance."

Regardless of their orthographical expertise, their accomplishments have muted any criticism as to whether they could spell well or good; or both? Is it potato or potatoe?

NO PRESIDENT CAN SERIOUSLY INJURE THE GOVERNMENT

Starting with Washington we have accepted the outcome of the ballot box, trusting that its temporary occupant in the White House cannot corrupt the system to any damaging degree in four years. Our presidents have, for the most part, kept the faith as established by good old George and the Constitution, and even the worst of them did little damage. The only time a minority refused to accept this outcome led to our bloodiest war.

Never was a more reasonable articulation of this point made, justifying reliance on our system, than that of the following brief paragraph in Abe Lincoln's First Inaugural Address:

"While the people retain their virtue, and vigilance, no administration, by any extreme of wickedness of folly, can very seriously injure the government, in the short space of four years."

THERE IS NO DIVIDING LINE

The following quotation from Lincoln is the most eloquent argument ever made against the breakup of our Union:

"...A nation may be said to consist of its territory, its people and its laws. The territory is the only part which is of certain durability. 'One generation passeth away, and another generation cometh, but the earth abideth forever.'...That portion of the earth's surface which is owned and inhabited by the people of the United States is suited for one national family...it is not well adapted for two or more...Physically speaking, we cannot separate. We cannot remove our respective sections from each other, nor build an inseparable wall between them. A husband and wife may be divorced (and go their separate ways), but the different parts of the country cannot do this...intercourse...must continue between them...Can aliens make treaties easier than friends make laws? Can treaties be more faithfully enforced between aliens, than laws can among friends? So you go to war, you cannot fight always; and when, after much loss on both sides, and no gain on either, you cease fighting, the same old questions as to terms of intercourse, are again upon you. There is no line, straight or crooked, suitable for a national boundary, upon which to divide...Our national strife springs not from our territory...Our strife pertains to ourselves—-to the passing generations of men; and it can, without convulsion, be hushed forever with the passing of one generation..."

And it came to pass in one generation.

State of the Union Address, 12/01/62.

COUNT PEEPER'S DISGRACE

The Cutts affair reveals the quixotic character and concerned response of Abe Lincoln regarding an event or incident. Captain James Cutts, brother-in-law of Stephen A. Douglas, was court martialed for conduct unbecoming an officer and for peeping through a keyhole and transom to watch a young lady undress. He was found guilty and thrown out of the army. An appeal was made to Abe to intervene and give Cutts his rank back.

When Abe first heard of the incident, he privately quipped that Cutts "should be elevated to the peerage with the title of Count Peeper." Due to the seriousness of the matter and out of respect for his old friend, he did intervene. Captain Cutts was called in and reprimanded by Abe, who then restored his rank.

KILLING THE DOG WON'T CURE THE BITE

After Abe dismissed Cutts, he wrote him a most beautiful letter. A quote taken from it competes with Solomon's best. "No man resolved to make the most of himself, can spare time for personal contention...Better give your path to a dog, than be bitten by him in contending for the right. Even killing the dog will not cure the bite."

The cynical might say that Abe paid off a debt to an old friend, but rather than destroy the offender he chose to give the man a second chance. Again, Abe's talent at judging character was exonerated, for Captain Cutts distinguished himself in combat and twice therafter received the Congressional Medal of Honor.

LANE'S SALT AND PEPPER JAYHAWKERS

Senator James H. Lane, was an ardent abolitionist and good friend of old John Brown. They had fought together in the struggle to make Kansas a free state and had encouraged slave men to run away and fight for their freedom with white abolitionists.

Early on, Lane had black and white men fighting together. *"The Leavenworth Daily Conservative"* of October 6, 1861, observed that Lane's forces contained black and white cavalrymen riding side by side. Throughout the war there were other instances where black and white Kansas men fought together.

Although officially opposing the arming of black slaves at that stage of the Civil War, Abe knew about Lane and appointed him a brigadier general in 1861. The President knew that Lane would do everything in his power to defeat the South, including recruiting and training black soldiers.

PRESIDENTIAL CORNS

In later life, Abe's feet constantly hurt from corns and a painful bunion. Although bunions can be hereditary, most of them and corns are the result of poorly fitting shoes and abuse. Abe's were no doubt the product of the poverty of his youth and young adulthood.

After becoming president, Abe was intro-duced to a young chiropodist, Isachar Zacharie, an English Jew. Lincoln utilized his services and had such a high regard for Zacharie's work that he gave a written testi-monial for the young chiropodist. The satirists had their day. The *New York Herald* said, "Dr.Zacharie has made his debut on the national stage to cut the Presidential corns."

ON MARFAN SYNDROME

Occasionally, a sensational article appears in the tabloids and similar publications proving conclusively that Abe Lincoln suffered from Marfan Syndrome and would have soon died had he not been assassinated by John Wilkes Booth. The disease is a hereditary disorder principally affecting the connective tissues of the body, manifested in varying degrees by excessive bone elongation and joint flexibility and by abnormalities of the eye and cardiovascular system. This position is based upon Abe's physical appearance and the fatigue he suffered near the end of his life.

Modern historical and medical research concludes that the available evidence does not indicate that Abe suffered from Marfan syndrome. Furthermore, he appeared to be in great shape after his visit to City Point, Virginia, in late March of '65. (See OLD ABE WASN'T THAT OLD AFTER ALL)

COOPER UNION AT LEAVENWORTH

Abe was most aware of the importance of his speech to be given before the Young Men's Republican Union of New York City on February 27, 1860, at Cooper Union Hall. His performance in the Lincoln-Douglas debates had made him a national figure. His book of the debates, published in fifty-nine, was popular and had kept his name before the public. Invitations to speak flowed in to Springfield, many being turned down. Republicans wanted to see and hear him, especially on the east coast and in New England. His name was being mentioned as a presidential candidate. If he played it right, his appearance at Cooper Union would boost his chances for the presidential nomination.

As always, Abe arduously prepared for an important endeavor. After working hard on his manuscript, he went out to Leavenworth, Kansas in early December of fifty-nine and made four talks—a nice place to refine his speech and practice his lines in the boon docks and away from reporters from the big east coast newspapers. Lincoln was probably the first aspirant for the nomination of his political party to do this. Like modern day candidates, he perfected the speech on the grass roots. The method worked, and Lincoln's Cooper Union Address was a smashing success and contributed greatly to his procuring the nomination.

THE MAN I'M BEHIND

Abe was always concerned about people, regardless of their station in life. He made a practice of shaking hands with men and women in common, hard working occupations. Whenever he made a trip, he would, if at all possible, seek out the firemen and engineers on steamboats or trains and share a few words with them and a friendly handshake. Many times the workers apologized for their dirty hands and unkept appearances resulting from the job.

These never bothered Abe.

A conductor once asked him, "Why do you always bother shaking hands with the engineer and fireman, whose hands are always covered with soot and grease?"

Abe answered, "That will wash off, but I always want to see and know the men I am riding behind."

IN MEMORIAM

In November, '61, Steve Douglas died. The North found no more devoted supporter of the Union or of Lincoln than Stephen Douglas.

His second wife visited Lincoln later that month, concerned about the possibility that her children's lands and wealth located in the South might be confiscated as rebel contraband by the Union Army. He assured her that it would not be taken, and it wasn't.

SHOVELING FLEAS

McClellan was a cautious, "Nervous Nellie" type who was afraid to commit himself. He never had enough men and supplies and was constantly preparing to do battle, while Lee was prepared.

Abe said, "Sending men to him was like trying to shovel fleas across a barnyard; not half of them got there,"and, "If I gave him all the men he wanted, the Army of the Potomac could not lie down. It would have to sleep standing up!"

IT'S FAMILY, ABE

When Lincoln became President, he gave many of his old friends in Springfield government jobs. One of the recipients was Ninian Edwards, long time political ally and brother-in-law. He was appointed to the lucrative position of Commissary for the U.S. Army.

For nearly two years, Abe received numerous complaints from old friends charging that Ninian had used his position for personal gain. This caused much embarrassment to the President, and he was forced to remove Edwards from the position, because he would not straighten up his act.

Living Lincoln, 556-7; War Years, 61-64. 256.

BEAN POLES AND CORN STALKS

The Civil War saw the emergence of the telegraph and the railroads as vital cogs in the war effort and objects for destruction. Stonewall Jackson, Jeb Stuart and Nathan Bedford Forrest were masters at disrupting the Union's transportation facilities, and Phil Sheridan and Billy Sherman returned the favor to the South.

Breakthroughs in railroad building by Union army engineers were amazing. Eventually they could rebuild railroad bridges and tracks almost as fast as the rebels could destroy them. General Herman Haupt and his engineers rebuilt a 100 feet high by 400 feet wide railroad bridge over Potomac Creek in less that forty hours. Haupt was Lincoln's kind of general: Short on talk, tall on works and always ready! Abe remarked that although he was a brigadier general, Haupt had the brains of a major general. Both greatly admired each other.

Describing the army engineers' work Abe said, "Every day heavily loaded trains pass over these bridges, and they look like nothing but so many bean poles and corn stalks."

PLEASE SEND HOME MY LOVER FOR I NEEDTH A HUSBAND

Abe received a letter from a Quaker girl in Pennsylvania in early '64, giving ",,,a brief history connected with myself and would be husband." They had been engaged for some years, when he enlisted for three years in the army. Her lover was given a furlough in October, '63, to go home and vote. "...It was our design to marry while he was at home and under those determina- tions we very foolishly indulged in matrimonial affairs..."She named the outfit of the father of her unborn child and requested that he be sent home so that they could be married.

Across the back of the letter, Lincoln wrote to the Secretary Of War; "Send him to her by all means."

DON'T SHOOT, SPANK

A little known aspect of the Civil War is the large number of children who actively participated in the bloody struggle. If a youth were large for his age, recruiters asked no questions and signed him up. This resulted in preteenage boys being inducted into the army. Many of these children were company mascots, and others served as drummer or bugle boys. They were exposed to the same hardships and horrors of war as adults, and many were killed in combat, especially drummer and bugle boys. Messages were sent to men in battle by bugle calls and drum rolls. This function was most important and made them the targets of enemy sharp shooters.

Occasionally, a boy became a hero and the subject of popular war ballads. Johnny Clem was ten when he ran away from home and became a mascot of the 22nd Massa-

chusetts. The men gave him a sawed-off musket, a petite uniform and chipped in his pay until he officially became a soldier in 1863. He was at Shiloh and, at the tender age of twelve, shot and killed a Confederate colonel at Chickamauga. For a time Clem was a prisoner of war.

These youths were also subject to the same brutal discipline as men, and some were even sentenced to death for infractions of military law. When Lincoln learned that fourteen year old drummer boy, Daniel Winger, was to be shot for going to sleep while on guard duty, Abe pardoned him and sent Secretary Of War, Edwin Stanton, the following letter:

"Hadn't we better spank this drummer boy and send him home to Leavenworth?"

MARY'S EMPLOYMENT BUREAU

Besides being hostess of the White House, Mary spent time as a volunteer at the Army Hospitals caring for the wounded soldiers. She also wished to see slavery abolished and helped the contraband slaves. These poor people faced enumerable hardships and were in desperate need. As dependent servants and field workers, they had little or no experience in caring for themselves. They possessed few job skills and had very little knowledge about finding work. Abolitionists, free northern blacks and many churches established charitable organizations, medical societies and schools for the contrabands.

Lizzie Keckley, Mary Lincoln's black seamstress and close friend, founded one of the first contraband aid societies in the country. Mrs. Lincoln supported Liz in this endeavor, and Abe gave money. Mary also became a "one woman employment bureau" for these poor black people in Washington D.C., doing what she could to find them jobs.

GOD'S WILL

Throughout his years in the White House Abe was constantly subjected to the opinions of ministers advising him to carry out their recommendations, because they represented divine will. At times these opinions were diametrically opposed, prompting him to write: "I am approached with the most opposite opinions and advice, and that by religious men who are equally certain that they represent the divine will. I am sure that either the one or the other class is mistaken in that belief...I hope it will not be irreverent for me to say that if it is probable that God would reveal his will to others on a point so connected with my duty, it might be supposed he would reveal it directly to me; for, unless I am more deceived in myself than I often am, it is my earnest desire to know the will of Providence in this matter. And if I can learn what it is, I will do it."

IT'S FAMILY, BROTHER LINCOLN

In 1863, Mary Lincoln was in deep depression from the loss of her son, Willie. Her sister, Emily Helm, had lost her husband about the same time. Both women were in deep grief, and Abe encouraged Emily to visit them at the White House. He hoped it would cheer up Mary, who deeply cared for Emily and her late husband, Ben.

At the end of her visit, Abe wrote a pass for Emily to protect her return to her home in Kentucky. Following her return, she became involved in certain disloyal activities, and the Union commander, General Burbridge, attempted to arrest her. Emily used Abe's pass to escape arrest. When notified of this action, Lincoln wrote Burbridge, withdrawing the pass and instructing him to treat her just like any other person.

HULLO, MASSA! BOTTOM RAIL ON TOP!

Leslies's Weekly reported a black man took a hand in a guerrilla fight: We fit 'em, we whopt 'em and we kotched ten uv 'em." By late '62, many slaves and free blacks became an active part of the army. The status of the blacks changed, and so did the attitude and bearing of the former slaves.

Harper's Monthly told of Confederate prisoners at Rock Island, Illinois, under Negro guards. One guard, suddenly seeing his former master as a prisoner cried out, "Hullo, massa! Bottom rail on top!"

A SAD, SWEET FAREWELL

"MY FRIENDS –
NO ONE, NOT IN MY SITUATION, CAN APPRECIATE MY FEELING OF SADNESS AT THIS PARTING. TO THIS PLACE, AND THE KINDNESS OF THESE PEOPLE, I OWE EVERYTHING. HERE I HAVE LIVED A QUARTER OF A CENTURY, AND HAVE PASSED FROM A YOUNG TO AN OLD MAN. HERE MY CHILDREN HAVE BEEN BORN AND ONE IS BURIED. I NOW LEAVE, NOT KNOWING WHEN, OR WHETHER EVER, I MAY RETURN, WITH A TASK BEFORE ME GREATER THAN THAT WHICH RESTED UPON WASHINGTON. WITHOUT THE ASSISTANCE OF THAT DIVINE BEING, WHOEVER ATTENDED HIM, I CANNOT SUCCEED. WITH THAT ASSISTANCE, I CANNOT FAIL. TRUSTING IN HIM, WHO CAN GO WITH ME, AND REMAIN WITH YOU AND BE EVERYWHERE FOR GOOD, LET US CONFIDENTLY HOPE THAT ALL WILL YET BE WELL. TO HIS CARE COMMENDING YOU, AS I HOPE IN YOUR PRAYERS YOU WILL COMMEND ME, I BID YOU AN AFFECTIONATE FAREWELL."

When Abe departed Springfield to go to Washington on February 11, 1861, he delivered one of his outstanding pieces. It is classic Lincoln, simple, brief, honest, and devoid of the typical bravado usually displayed by leaders in similar circumstances. By today's standards," he let it all hang out."

In those few words he covered the major events in a quarter of a century of his life and his relationships with the community and those persons who were dear to him. Wishing to assure, yet honest enough to reveal to his friends and to the world his trepidation about the immense task facing him, Lincoln expressed his confidence in finding an ultimate solution to a divided nation in Him Who knows and controls all. He opined that with God's help he could win; without it, he would fail. This appeal for God's help in such a forthright manner was accepted by the American people. Such public honesty wears well and remains dear to us.

HE WOULD HAVE DIED YEARS AGO

Abe's quick wit could be spontaneous, clever and occasionally a bit caustic. He once commented to David R. Locke, the creator of Petroleum Nasby and one of his favorite writers, about a deceased politician of inordinate vanity, "If General— had known how big a funeral he would have had, he would have died years ago."

RE-LIERS

Today, very few Americans can imagine the nature and quantity of the vilifying and intensely critical newspaper coverage of Abe. Such terms as baboon and gorilla were complimentary. This quote taken from the February 25, 1865, issue of the *Leslie's Weekly* is typical: "There is no man of less consequence in these United States than Abraham Lincoln of Illinois. A school boy would deserve flogging for sending out documents of such prodigious moment as come from his pen in phrases so mean and unbe-

coming." Like water and the proverbial duck, it rolled off his back.

One day Secretary of the Navy Gidean Wells' wife mentioned similar malignant reports in the newspapers regarding the President and the fact that they were not telling the truth about his administration. "The papers are not always reliable," Abe interjected. "That is to say, Mrs. Wells, they lie and then they relie".

War Years, 1-4, 346, 768.

A DRY PLACE TO BE

By the fifties Lincoln & Herndon was regarded as one of the leading law firms in Springfield. Lincoln's third, best and most enduring partner was Billy Herndon who described their general law practice as involving no very large principal and rewarding with no very large fee. The firm appeared before Justices of the Peace and the Illinois Supreme Court; it handled "ten cent" cases and major railroad suits. Philosophcally, Billy wrote, "A law office is a very dry place for incident of a pleasing kind. If you love the stories of murder—rape—fraud, etc.(,) a law office is a good place..."

Abe had a different view about their practice. He enjoyed the law and helping people. All cases were important. A squabble over a lit-ter of pigs might be a trifling matter to some, but it was most important to the party involved. As a rule Abe interviewed the client, explained his options and wrote up the papers if a case were initiated. During this meeting Abe invariably had to tell a joke which was always followed with boisterous laughter by both parties. These jokes and Lincoln's reaction to them mystified Hern-don. The constant re-telling of them irritated Billy, and he could never understand his partner's laughing at the joke as if he had never heard it before..

Abe was the senior partner whose warmth, concern and success attracted most of the clients. Rumor had it that Billy did the read-ing and Lincoln did the thinking for the firm.

FRIEND DOUGLASS

Abe was the first president to allow black persons access to the chief executive. Early in the Lincoln Administration, Frederick Douglass discovered that black leaders were welcome at the White House. Although he disagreed with many of Abe's policies, personally he greatly admired Lincoln.

"He treated me as a man. The first white man (to do so)", Douglass told a friend. Continuing, "... He did not let me feel for a moment that there was any difference in the color of our skins. The President is a most remarkable man!"

War Years, 307-9; Oates, 386, 447; Peterson, 59.

SORE TONGUED HORSES

Lincoln put up with a lot of dawdling, at times bordering on insolence, from General McClellan in hopes of obtaining a sound victory. Following the Union's second defeat at Bull Run in August of '62, Abe reinstated "Little Mac" as commander of the Army of the Potomac.,

With a little dash he could have turned his lackluster showing at Antietam into a great military victory for the Union. Lee was trapped in Maryland by the flooding Potomac River, was without supplies and was a sitting duck, had McClellan taken advantage of the situation. But as usual, "Mac" hesitated and failed to take the initiative. In a letter to Abe, he justified his inaction on account of "fatigued and sore tongued horses."

Distraught at the failed opportunity to win a decisive victory, Lincoln in a rare display of sarcasm wrote, "Will you pardon me for asking what the horses of your army have done since the Battle of Antietam that fatigues anything?"

DOLL JACK

Even with the most taxing schedule, Lincoln did spend some time with his children. One day Tad and Willie Lincoln, accompanied by their little friends, Bud and Holly Taft, caught the Zouave doll, Jack, asleep on guard duty, court martialed him and took him out to the rose garden to be shot and buried. They felt bad about having to do away with Jack, and the gardener overheard them talking.

"Well," he said, "Why don't you go see the President and ask him for a pardon. Then you won't have to shoot him. Maybe, he'll give you one. He gives them to everybody else!"

Sure enough, the boys went to the President's office and told him about Jack and asked for a pardon. Abe picked up a piece of White House stationery and wrote "Jack the Zouave Doll is pardoned. By order of the President A. LINCOLN." Four little boys charged out of his office thrilled that they didn't have to shoot their doll.

A few days later Jack was found hanging from a rose trellis by the neck. Apparently he had turned traitor and sold out to the Johnnie Rebs, and the boys had executed him.

A DEMOCRAT APPOINTED

From the time Abe became President Elect he was continually bombarded by Republican Party regulars and elected officials seeking government jobs. Most of the time he dispensed "the loaves and fishes" of patronage to faithful Republicans, but occasionally, he did appoint a Democrat, causing a hue and cry among the party faithful.

To the disgruntled Republicans he would humorously respond, "Occasionally, I must appoint a man that can get the job done!"

IT'S THE FORMS THAT COUNT

Lincoln made it his duty to see that the military had the most up-to-date weapons. An inventor himself, he loved to talk with persons who had designed new firearms. Many mornings he would fire these new weapons at his private range in Treasury Park beyond the south lawn of the White House.

In his effort to adopt new arms Lincoln was consistently hampered by the army bureaucracy, which was led by Chief of Ordinance, General James Ripley. The General was a traditionalist, who objected to every new idea and opposed the breech loading rifle, the re-peating rifle, the "coffee-mill"(machine) gun and virtually every other military novelty.

In October of '61, Lincoln ordered Ripley to purchase 25,000 Marsh breech loaders for the army. The order was not executed. In December, Abe discovered his request had not been carried out and personally saw to it that the army got Spencer breech loading rifles. Ripley's excuse for not purchasing the rifles was that he figured the war would soon be over, and they would not be needed. Besides, his office would have the extra work of changing its order forms.

Oates, 264; Lincoln, 431.

UNDUE PREPARATION

Another of Abe's favorite stories, which he used to motivate the cautious and timid in his administration to get off the dime, was the fable of the man who over prepared.

"One day a man was travelling on foot across unfamiliar country, carrying his possessions in a bundle. He came to a stream, and, not knowing the depth of the river he was about to ford, he made elaborate preparations for his crossing. Stripping off his garments and adding them to his bundle, he bound them together and tied his belongings to the end of a stick. This would enable him to hold his possessions high over his head to prevent them from getting wet during the crossing. He then fearlessly waded in and carefully made his way across the rippling stream, only to discover that the water at no place covered his ankles."

THE FACE ON THE PENNY

As Abe's one hundreth birthday approached, President Theodore Roosevelt, a great admirer of Lincoln, supported the idea of a coin honoring the 16th President. Thus was issued the first United States coin to honor a president, the 1909 Lincoln penny. The familiar portrait by Victor Brenner is said to be the most reproduced picture in the world.

As a part of his 150th birthday anniversay in 1959, the United States Mint redesigned the reverse side of the penny by impressing an engraving of the Lincoln Memorial.

THOSE COPPERHEADS

During the Civil War some Northerners expressed pro South sentiment. They believed in allowing the South to secede from the Union and were opposed to the war. They were called copperheads after the vicious pit viper that thrives in the hill country of the Mississippi Valley. The most celebrated leader of the copperheads was Democratic Congressman, Clement Vallandigham.

This element, most of them anti war or peace Democrats, caused all kinds of trouble, including encouraging soldiers to desert. Many young men followed their advice and were court martialed and sentenced to be executed for desertion. This caused Abe much pain and grief and prompted him to write, "Must I shoot a simple-minded soldier boy who deserts, while I must not touch a hair of a wily agitator who induces him to desert...I think that in such a case, to silence the agitator, and save the boy, is not only constitutional, but withal, a great mercy."

Lincoln's feelings on this particular situation was responsible for many of the pardons he granted to those condemned to be shot for desertion.

IF IT WEREN'T FOR MENTOR GRAHAM

One of the more popular Lincoln stories told at gatherings of educators and school commencement exercises regards Abe's New Salem school teacher friend, Mentor Graham. Its telling gives teachers a warm cuddly feeling about their profession and its contributions to students.

Supposedly, Graham was at Lincoln's inauguration— actually seated with Mary, Steve Douglas and the other guests of honor. As Abe delivered his address, a member of the crowd said to a friend. "There sits Mentor Graham. If it weren't for Abraham Lincoln, he wouldn't be there.'

"Yes," said his colleague, "And, if it weren't for Mentor Graham, Abe wouldn't be there!"

Without doubt, the Scottish schoolmaster certainly did help Abe and shared his intellectual interests. Graham encouraged him to undertake the study of grammar and public speaking, and for a time in 1833, Lincoln lived at the Graham house in New Salem. According to the only biography of Mentor Graham, by Duncan and Nickols, Graham was present at the inauguration. Some historians have questioned their research. It is one of the Lincoln tales that just might be too good to be true, but teachers love it.

AS ABE SOWED IN '58

In the great Lincoln-Douglas Debates of 1858, Abe injected a moral issue regarding slavery. He consistently argued that slavery was wrong, but he would tolerate its existence in the slave states until some method of gradual, peaceful emancipation could be arranged. However, under no condition or circumstance would he allow its extension into the territories of the United States. The evil of slavery must be contained and eventually done away with, for no nation could long remain half slave, half free!

     Jaffa, 404; Quarles 138; Oates, 324.

SO HE REAPED IN '62

In December of 1861, the Republicans elected with Lincoln acquired control of the Congress. During the summer of '62, Lincoln signed two important pieces of legislation on slavery passed by that congress. On April 16, '62, slavery was abolished within Washington, and on the following June 12th, it was forbidden in the territories. According to the Supreme Court, such legislation was unconstitutional, and yet little was made about that issue. Less than three months later, Lincoln would issue his preliminary Emancipation Proclamation, which he officially proclaimed on the following New Year's Day.

According to Scripture, we are told, "As ye sow, so shall ye reap," and that's exactly what happened with Old Abe. In our history good politicians keep their promises, and Abe was a good one.

I'SE CONTRABAND

From the beginning of the Civil War, the Lincoln Administration had a problem with what to do about slaves acquired by the army in combat or those that surrendered to it after fleeing their masters. What was their status? Were they free? Were they to be returned to their masters? Were they contraband of war to be treated like any other property taken from the enemy and not returned?

Complicating this problem was how to keep the four remaining slave states within the Union. Since many of these slave owners were loyal, they were not to be treated the same as those planters who supported the rebels. It was not fair to the Border States to take their valuable property from them. Early in the war General Benjamin Butler declared these slaves contraband of the Union government, and Abe reluctantly allowed Butler's position of declaring these slaves contraband to become precedent. Within a very short time, southern slaves learned about this policy. Henceforth, wherever units of the Union Army invaded Confederate territory, large numbers of slaves ran away from their masters and penetrated northern military lines to become contrabands.

OUR FIRST FIRST LADY

Mary Lincoln achieved some successes on her own as mistress of the White House and was the most noteworthy female to reside in that structure since Dolly Madison. Having learned politics from her father and Henry Clay, she was politically astute and had been involved with Abe's politics even before they were married. Mary had no intention of fading quietly into the woodwork. She would be the First Lady of the country—a term that was fashioned to describe her.

She enjoyed the role as hostess and made a favorable impression. Her major project was redecorating the White House, which was in a rundown condition upon her arrival. It had the appearance of a third rate motel and had not been refurbished in years. When she departed the Mansion, it was sparkling clean, beautifully furnished and a residence befitting the President of the United States of America. She was our first First Lady.

GET DOWN, YOU DAMNED FOOL!

Remembered history is always filled with myth, but it is a wonderful source of stories of the past that give color, warmth and inspiration to a people. Associate Justice Oliver Wendel Holmes, Jr. is the only source of this story, which he frequently told to the amusement of many. The judge was proud of his Civil War record and was wounded four times in battle. Holmes was not like so many young men of wealth, who legally shirked their responsibility to fight in the Civil War by buying a substitute or applying some other subterfuge to avoid the army.

The only time he ever saw Abe was at the battle of Fort Stevens during the summer of 1864. In his eagerness to see the battle, Lincoln exposed himself to enemy fire. Capt. Holmes, not realizing who the civilian was at that moment, yelled at the tall spectator, "Get down, you damned fool, before you get shot!" Lincoln quickly complied with the officer's order. Only then did Holmes recognize the object of his abrupt command. The young officer, aghast at his oversight, did not know what to expect when hostilities ceased.

After the battle was over and the enemy had withdrawn, Abe came up to the chagrined young captain, shook his hand and laughingly said, "You are the only military man I ever met that knows how to talk to a politician."

KNOWING HOW TO TALK TO A POLITICIAN

LOOKING UP AT THE HEAVENS

Abe was a very devout man who studied the *Bible* diligently, prayed frequently, attended church regularly, and believed in God as a Supreme Being who endowed people with individual destinies. In a conversation during the summer of '64 with his good friend Josh Speed he counselled, "...Speed, take all of this *Book* upon reason that you can, and the balance on faith, and you will live and die a happier man." His faith came from the *Bible.*

Since his theology did not require that he be a member of a particular church, he never professed to be a Christian. This lack of church membership was not unique, for in his day even serious Christians did not automatically join a church. Only about 23 per-cent of the population of this country were church members in 1860. The idea that it was impossible to be a Christian alone and that it is only in the gathered fellowship of a church that Christ is truly known was not very popular.

Abe also found God in nature as revealed in the following fragment:

"I can see how a man might look down on the face of the earth and be an atheist, but I can not conceive how he can look up at the heavens and believe that there is no God."

FATAL FLAW?

Abe believed in obeying the law and strongly supported the Constitution and the individual rights it contained. However, because of the unique circumstances resulting from the Civil War, he felt compelled to issue an executive order suspending the Writ of Habeas Corpus, which is our greatest protection from an oppressive police state.

He was faced with resolving the dilemma of how to reconcile minority rights with the practice of representative government based upon majority rule.

According to many experts, he was the closest thing to a military dictator this nation ever had. Temporarily, he did wield dictatorial power but backed away from it or got the Congress to uphold such urgent actions by law. Because of his sterling humanity, lawyerly caution, and absence of malice, Abe never became a dictator.

200,000 STRONG FOR FREEDOM

From the beginning of the Civil War, black men had wanted to fight for the Union as they had in the wars of independence against England. By the war's end, they would compose nearly ten percent of the Union Army, approximately 200,000, or equal to the total number of Confederate troops when it surrendered in April of '65.

Black courage and valor on the battlefield prompted the earliest expressions of black pride and manhood, Their love of Old Abe is evidenced by the verse taken from the "Marching Song of the First of Arkansas (Negro) Regiment", set to the tune of "John Brown's Body." With the exception of the first line of the song, the words are those of Sojourner Truth, black poet, aboltionist, underground railroad guide and leader for black and women's rights. She first sang it for a black Michigan regiment during the Thanksgiving celebration of 1863. Like the First of Arkansas, many other black outfits adopted her words and the tune for their marching song.

Since less than one percent of the North's population was black, most of the black soldiers had been southern slaves. They overcame generations of servility and served the Union with distinction. Twenty three were recipients of the Congressional Medal of Honor. The names of these recipients can be found on page 185 of Gladstone's *Men of Color*.

166   Oates, 386; War Years, 307-9, 577; Burns, 248-252; Newhouse, 177-78.

A FLATULENT MEDIUM

Lincoln had an abiding interest in new weapons which might help end the war. He collected models of these inventions. Frequently, he had Admiral John Dahlgren test and demonstrate these new machines of destruction.

One day, Lincoln, Seward, Stanton and a correspondent of the *New York Tribune* observed Dahlgren successfully test a French repeating rifle-—a machine gun—at the Washington Naval Yard. Afterward, Dahlgren explained how the firing mechanism operated by preventing the escape of the gas at the breach.

With a mischievous glance at the reporter, Abe said, "Now have any of you heard of any machine, or invention, for preventing the escape of 'gas' from the newspaper establishments?" Touche'!

Lincoln, 431-32.

FOXHOLES MAKE COWARDS

Early in the war Confederate generals ordered their men to dig in to protect themselves from artillery and rifle fire. The Union generals were reluctant to adopt this practice, because, according to their military tactics and thinking, it might cause the men to fear death more.

Any man with enough sense to pound sand in a rat hole knew better, and so did Abe.

PAY A MAN HIS WAGE

A poor widow, Mrs. Baird, had a son in the army, who for some offense was sentenced to serve a long time without pay. The money was the sole source of Mrs. Baird's income, which she needed to survive. She had appealed to Abe for help, and he had written her a letter ordering the Army to make adjustments to help the penniless widow.

When she later informed him that the army had not acted on his direction, he wrote the following to Secretary of War, Stanton:

"I do not like this punishment of withholding pay—it falls so very hard on the poor... At the appeal of the poor mother, I made a direction that he be allowed to enlist for a new term, on the same conditions as others. She now comes, and says that she cannot get it acted upon. PLEASE DO IT!

A Lincoln."

It was acted upon!

A BUZZARD'S HEART

Politicians see the best and worst of human behavior displayed on a daily basis. Someone is always wanting something from them which is neither immoral or greedy but an expression of the constitutional right to petition. The common man is direct and to the point and lacks the discreet techniques and guile displayed by the sophisticated and polished. Abe understood this procedure very well, and, at times, his tart humor impaled the highborne and mighty.

One day a group of bankers came to see him to negotiate a large government loan which would make them a lot of money.

One of the bankers chirped, "You know, Mr. President, where the treasure is, there will be the heart also."

Abe, not being able to ignore this smug justification of greed, retorted, "I should wonder if another text would not fit the case better, 'Where the carcass is, there will be the buzzards gathered together.'"

HALF PAY

Initially, black soldiers were paid half the wages of comparable ranked whites in the army. Frederick Douglass personally complained to Lincoln about this matter as being unfair. Abe agreed with him but said that sometimes "…we have to make some concession to prejudice." He further assured Douglas that in due time, black soldiers would receive the same benefits.

In 1864, Lincoln urged the Congress to correct this inequity, and "technically" it did.

Oates, 386; War Years, 307-9.

USING THEIR JAWS MORE THAN THEIR BRAINS

One day, Jay Cooke, Union Civil War Financier, made a holiday visit with Lincoln and members of his cabinet. Cooke's Father had solid black hair without a gray hair in it and a pure white beard and mustache. Attorney General Bates's hair and beard was much the same. Upon seeing Bates, Cooke asked, why such a phenomenon took place?

With a bemused look at Bates, Abe responded, "Oh, Mr. Cooke, that is easily accounted for."

"I shall be glad to know the reason."

"Well, it could hardly be otherwise. The cause is that he uses his jaws more than he does his brains."

SWEARS LIKE A CHURCH WARDEN

Lincoln probably made himself the butt of his jokes more often than any other person. At times, he turned on his cabinet members, and no one was immune from his humorous barbs.

One day, while riding around the army camps in a mule drawn ambulance, he became amused at his driver. The soldier cursed everything with a flourish—the mules, the weather, the mud, the cavalry that sloshed by, etc. Finely Abe couldn't resist and tapped him on the shoulder, "Excuse me, my friend, are you an Episcopalian?"

"No," the driver replied, "I'm a Methodist. Why, sir?"

"Well," Lincoln said, "I thought you were an Episcopalian, because you swear just like Governor Seward, who is a church warden."

Oates, 373.

HOW LONG SHOULD A MAN'S LEGS BE?

It is a rare speaker, minister, writer, or teacher who has not at some time in their career used the Lincoln quote about the length of a man's legs. As popular as it is, there is little valid historical evidence to substantiate it. But we all have laughed at its telling, and for the sake of tradition, here it is again.

"Mr President, How long should a man's legs be?"

Abe, "Long enough to reach from his hips to the ground."

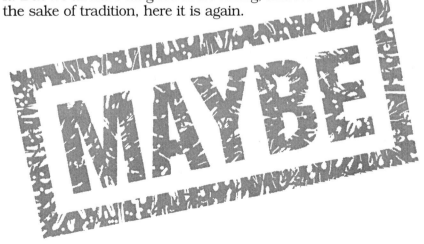

DEAR FANNY LETTER

Dear Fanny,

It is with deep grief that I learn of the death of your kind and brave father; and, especially, that it is affecting your young heart beyond what is common in such cases. In this sad world of ours, sorrow comes to all; and, to the young, it comes with bitterest agony, because it takes them unawares. The old have learned to ever expect it. I am anxious to afford some alleviation of your present distress. Perfect relief is not possible, except with time. You cannot now realize that you will ever feel better. Is it not so? And yet it is a mistake. You are sure to be happy again. To know this, which is certainly true, will make you some less miserable now. I have had experience enough to know what I say; and you need only to believe it, to feel better at once. The memory of your dear father, instead of an agony, will yet be a sad sweet feeling in your heart, of a purer, and holier sort than you have ever known before.

Please present my kind regards to your afflicted mother.

Your sincere friend
A. Lincoln—

Fanny McCullough and her sister were children of William McCullough, long time friend and clerk of the McLean County Circuit Court at Bloomington, Illinois. When on the circuit, Abe frequently stayed at the McCullough home and became friends with the girls. The children liked the tall, funny lawyer, and they became close friends. He held them on his lap, told them stories and gave them a good night kiss when they went to bed. "These little girls ain't too big to kiss," he often said.

Fanny's Father volunteered to fight for the Union and was killed during the Battle of Shiloh near Coffeeville, Mississippi. Learning of her intense anguish, he wrote her one of the most beautiful letters ever written to a person suffering such intense grief over the loss of a loved one. Selections from the McCullough letter appear on many sympathy cards. Under no circumstance should this be done, because the deletion of one word from this simple and sincere masterpiece detracts from its beauty. *SEE LETTERS.

PINING FOR ANN

The world loves a lover. Romance, especially of the high born and the famous, captivates and titillates the popular fancy. Such has been the case of the supposed Ann Rutledge-Abe Lincoln romance.

The principal source of this affair was Billy Herndon's biography of Lincoln. His motives for publicizing the romance have been questioned. Billy and Mary Lincoln were bitter enemies, and historians have suggested that he wrote about this imagined love affair to get back at her. Ironically, they knew Abe better than any other persons.

Herndon did an admirable job collecting material about Abe, which has helped the historian, but he possessed neither the discipline nor talent of one. As a lawyer, his pas-

sion for the truth went only so far— enough to win a case while not necesarily telling the whole truth.

In the late 1920's, a San Diego writer, Wilma Minor, convinced the respected "Atlantic Monthly Magazine" that she had original documents and love letters proving the romance had happened. The editor fell for it and thus set himself up for one of the most humiliating fiascoes in the history of magazine publication when the documents were proven to be forgeries.

Herndon's so called love affair has inspired poets, novelists, play rights and screen writers and, in all probability, will continue to do so, because the world loves a lover and romance.

Oates, 19-20, 31-2, 57; Peterson, 70-75, 291-2.

RIDICULE

Newspapers and magazines took delight in ridiculing Abe Lincoln. His physical appearance, manners, dialect and demeanor gave them ample opportunity for such sport. Shakespearean actor, James Hackett, allowed the press to print a letter from the president and was upset with their treatment of Lincoln. He wrote Abe a letter and apologized for any embarrassment or pain resulting from what he considered a thoughtless act.

In the following letter, Abe reassured Hackett not to worry, because he was accustomed to such treatment by the press:

"...I have not been much shocked by the newspaper comments upon it(letter). Those comments constitute a fair specimen of what has occurred to me through life. I have endured a great deal of ridicule without much malice; and have received a great deal of kindness, not quite free from ridicule, I am used to it."

THE PRAIRIE JANUS

Early in the Civil War Lincoln was most reluctant to officially support the arming of blacks in the army, realizing that he could lose the Border States to the Confederacy. When over zealous subordinates publicly encouraged or armed slaves, he officially disavowed their actions and sometimes removed them from their positions. However, he condoned and abetted such activities as long as neither he nor the public heard about it.

An example of this duplicitous behavior occurred in late June of '61 at the beginning of the war. While Lincoln assured gentlemen from the border state of Kentucky that slaves were not being recruited and armed by the US Army, he appointed Kansas Senator James Lane, an abolitionist friend of John Brown's, a brigadier general of volunteers, knowing that Lane was recruiting slaves for his regiment.

In a letter of June 20, 1861, to the Secretary of the Army Stanton, Abe subtly stated his position. "...I have been reflecting upon (Lane of Kansas), and have concluded that we need the services of such a man out there at once; that we better appoint him a brigadier-general of volunteers today, and send him off with such authority to raise a force...as you think will get him into actual work quickest. Tell him when he starts to put it through, Not be writing or telegraphing back here, but put it through."

So much for that old two faced story. Looks like Abe had two faces after all, and he did wear both of them.

THE SINS OF DANCING

One day, while visiting an army hospital, Abe came upon a young, wounded soldier who held in his weak, white hand a religious tract given to him by a well dressed lady intent on performing good works. Upon reading the title of the pamphlet, the soldier broke out in laughter, and the lady was standing nearby.

"Soldier." Abe said, "It is hardly fair to laugh at her gift. She meant no harm."

"I knows it, Mr. President," he replied, "but here she's a giv'en me this book called 'The Sins of Danc'n' and both of my legs is shot off!"

ABE'S SWEARER

A Boston man once said, "You never swear, Mister President, do you ?" With a chuckle Abe, replied, "Oh, I don't have to. You know I have Mr. Stanton in my Cabinet."

I WANT AN OFFIS.

One of Abe's favorite news commentators was the Ohio editor, David R. Locke, who went by the pen name of Petroleum V. Nasby. Locke wrote clever political satire, and Abe faithfully read it. He even offered him a job, which was declined.

Petroleum took pot shots at everybody including the President, but he had an affection for Lincoln as a man. This cartoon reflects Locke's concern for the President and at the same time, his contempt for incompetent, pompous, patriots endeavoring to sop at the public trough.

TOWERING GENIUS

It is a rare person who can compose a decent sentence. Abe Lincoln produced volumes of these gems. They were the product of his "blab school" education and his unique pattern of thought and observation, abetted by his prodigious memory. Sometimes, through misunderstanding or bias, they got him in trouble. In Abe's acceptance speech for the Senate in 1858, he said to his fellow Republicans, "I believe a government cannot stand half slave and half free." It was a typical Lincolnized adaptation of a quote found in the Bible—in three of the Gospels—and delivered for effect and not as a suggestion for action. However the southern slave interests didn't see that way, and it created a fire storm of protest.

At twenty-eight Abe said in his Lyceum Speech, "Towering genius disdains a beaten path". He was expressing his concern for the men who might become dissatisfied with the rewards available in our government and would overthrow it like Caesar. Imaginative 20th Century writers, known as revisionists, latched on to his argument and concluded that an overly ambitious Abe Lincoln secretly held similar views. They filled many a library shelf with this patriotic gore. Was their product scholarship or reading tea leaves?

Abe could have been suggesting the possibility of revolutions without leaders like George Washington as food for thought for a group of aspiring, young men in a little prairie town intent upon self improvement? Or, was it a disgruntled Whig smarting from the recent defeat of his party by Jackson Democrats, and, due to the non-partisan nature of the occasion, obliquely hinting at imagined excesses of King Andrew's Democrats? Politicians are always paranoid. Maybe young Lincoln was too close to our emerging pattern of restraint to see the forest of developing democratic tradition. He certainly contributed to that democratic tradition twenty-five years later. But Abe a subliminal Caesar? A latent Napoleon? WOW! This is a great quote composed by a young man with a sense of history; and history has revealed that wherever towering genius has trod, there have been new paths—most of them very beneficial.

Collected Works, 1, 108-15; Peterson, 382-83; Lincoln, 80-3.

DISDAINS A BEATEN PATH'

JEFF DAVIS' SUNSHINE PATRIOTS

It was the South which first adopted the draft and produced the first draft dodgers. Having a much smaller manpower base, the South initiated compulsory military service in April of 1862. By the war's end all able-bodied, white men from seventeen to fifty could be conscripted. "We are about to grind up the seed corn of the nation," Jeff Davis ruefully stated with its adoption.

The measure was hated more by the rebels than by the yankees. It was galling to strong states' rights men, who regarded conscription as another example of the central government trampling upon the individual's rights. Was that not the reason for secession? Furthermore, not every eligible man had to serve. Deferments were granted to those whose occupations were vital to the war effort: Railroad workers, miners, civil officials and teachers. (Many Confederate states experienced a booming interest in the teaching profession). Also despised was the so-called "twenty-negro" law which exempted the overseers of twenty or more slaves. Firebrand, patriotic sons of wealthy planters took the exemption and evaded military service. Equally onerous was the substitute provision, which allowed a wealthy man to hire the son of a poor farmer to do his fighting. As a substitute or a draftee, the poor were forced to fight and angrily resented the special treatment accorded the well-to-do. Many became our first draft dodgers.

Ironically, the Civil War draft dodger is rarely mentioned and never seen at today's Civil War re-enactments. At these romantic reproductions there are none of Jeff Davis' "sunshine patriots".

ABE LINCOLN'S SUMMERTIME SOLDIERS

In July of 1863, the Union implemented the draft. It was immensely unpopular. Besides its favoritism to the wealthy, Abe's shift from saving the union to include freeing the blacks angered many northerners. This unpopularity quickly led to the bloody draft riots of '63, with most of the violence being directed at innocent and defenseless urban blacks.

Allowing substitutes was detested as much in the North as it was in the South. Why should a man with three hundred dollars not go to war while the poor youth lacking funds had to fight? Why should the patriotic and the poor shed their blood while those with wealth could stay home and make a fortune? Thus the reluctant northern draftee, like his southern peer, became a draft dodger and hid out or fled to Canada. Abe was always opposed to the substitute provision, but even with Grant's and Sherman's urging, the Congress never did away with it. None of the members of the Harvard and Yale Rowing Teams of '64, served! One post Civil War president and all of those wealthy men known as the "Robber Barons" had substitutes. "A rich man's war and a poor man's fight," first heard in the South, was soon echoed in yankee land.

Later wars would eradicate the substitute mechanism from the draft, but educational, hardship and other types of deferments continued to allow the clever, the connected and the wealthy to legally avoid the draft. Not only Abe had "summertime soldiers"; all of our Twentieth Century war presidents had them as well. Ah, deja vu.

Oates, 387-388; War Years, 568-570; Burns, Civil War, 272.

AFTERMATH OF THE BATTLE OF GETTYSBURG

Both commanding generals at Gettysburg made serious mistakes, and under normal conditions they would have been removed from their commands. Lee's gallantry can never redeem the foolhardiness of his horrendous mistake in ordering Pickett's Charge up Cemetery Ridge, and Meade's serious error was in not capturing the battered Army of Northern Virginia following Gettysburg. The flooding Potomac River trapped Lee who was without supplies and helpless. Meade could have easily taken Lee's army and greatly altered the outcome of the war.

Both men tendered their resignations, but their superiors could not accept them because of the political situation. Jefferson Davis had little to repair the effect of Lee's folly but the charisma of the Lee mystique. Crowds of romantic southerners wildly cheered Bobby Lee following the defeat as if it were a victory. Ironically, the human sacrifice he foolishly ordered—Pickett's Charge—became a moment of honor and glory in the South. Davis' hands were tied. Lee had to remain.

Abe was in the same boat. His popularity was at its lowest ebb. The union had been defeated and humiliated for almost three years on the battlefield with a tremendous loss of life and limb. Lincoln had to have a victory to raise northern morale and to support his Emancipation Proclamation. To have fired Meade would have acknowledged defeat, and so Meade had to remain. Abe's genius was that he took that dubious Union victory and transformed the ugly reality of the battle into a pulpit for proclaiming the world's most beloved speech, the Gettysburg Address.

JUST CHARGE IT TO ME

A popular story about Lincoln's support of Grant made the rounds regarding the general's use of alcohol. Supposedly, a delegation of ministers called on the President complaining of Grant's drinking of hard liquor. When they finished, Abe asked them if they knew what the general's favorite brand of whiskey was, which prompted them to ask, "Why, Mr. President?"

"Oh, I'd just like to buy about 25 cases of his product and send it my generals who don't bring me victories."

When asked if the incident actually took place, Abe laughed, "That would have been very good if I had said it, but I guess you will just have to charge it to me to give it currency."

BEAST BUTLER'S ORDER(ly) LADIES

Ben Butler was probably the most despised yankee general in the post Civil War South. As the military governor of New Orleans in 1862, he was faced with a serious problem. The men of that city accepted the Union occupation, but the women did not. Though treated nicely by Butler's soldiers, they constantly insulted, threw human waste from their chamber pots, spit upon and even "mooned" yankee personnel.

Butler knew that to arrest these rebel heroines was very risky, but he could not tolerate their behavior. On May 15, 1862, Butler published Order 28."...any female who by word, gesture or movement, insulted or showed contempt for any Union soldier will be regarded and... treated as a woman of the town, plying her trade." The rebel ladies despised the order but conformed rather than be treated as harlots. Years later in his autobiography Butler noted that the ladies behaved themselves because they did not wish to be known as whores, and the whores behaved themselves because they wished to be considered ladies. However, those southern belles never forgave him, and he became the target of their vilest contempt. Long after Lee's surrender they continued hostilities by taking "pot shots" at Butler's portrait leering up from the inside bottom of their china chamber pots (Butler Thunder Mugs).

As a political general Butler was controversial and created problems for Lincoln. Occasioally Abe countermanded Butler's directives but he didn't intervene on Order 28.

Lowry, 151—153; Davis, 238.

I NEVER WALK BACK

From the preliminary announcement of the Emancipation Proclamation, September 22, 1862, until his death, Abe was continually urged by friends, important politicians and other influential people to reverse his position on freeing the blacks.

Politically the statement was harmful to him and the Republicans. In the fall elections of '62, the Democrats doubled their seats in Congress and won many important state offices. Until the summer of '64, the experts were sure Lincoln would be a one-term president, and the leaders of the Republican Party tried to dump him from the ticket. Besides his personal attitude about slavey, by that time he could not overlook the sacrifice and courage displayed by black men in

uniform. He was resolved to lose the election rather than back away from freeing the slaves.

Even after being re-elected in '64, he was still pressured to retract his position regarding the emancipation of the blacks. In his last State of the Union Address he wrote, "I repeat the declaration made a year ago, that 'while I remain in my present position I shall not attempt to retract or modify the Emancipation Proclamation, nor shall I return to slavery any person who is free by the terms of that proclamation, or by any of the acts of Congress'." Slow in making up his mind, he held according to his old axiom, "I may walk slow, but I don't walk back."

Oates, 367-8, 390, 429-31; Burns, 252; Living Lincoln, 633.

THE CHILDREN'S HOUR AT THE WHITE HOUSE

When the Lincolns moved into the Executive Mansion, their sons were a new experience for Americans,—children in the White House. The younger sons, Tad and Willie, had free run of the place, and they, along with their two special friends, Bud and Holly Taft, were into everything. The Taft boys' fifteen year old sister, Julia, was also a frequent visitor. When Abe could find the time, he enjoyed being with the children.

One day Julia heard a great commotion in the upstairs oval room. She entered and found the President of the United States lying on his back on the floor. Willie and Bud were holding down his legs, Tad and Holly his arms. "Julie, come quick and sit on his stomach!" cried Tad, as Abe struggled to free himself. Other times he would tell stories or read to them with the boys sitting upon him and his rocking chair.

THE PERFECT RAGE OF YOUTH

It seems that from the very beginning when Adam and Eve were able and raising cain there has been conflict between the parents and their offspring. Fortunately much of this strife is a part of growing up, but for many a talented, well-intentioned youth there exists a genuine basis for much of this unrest and a desire for experimentation and a thirst for what is new.

Abe was such a youth. He did not get along well with his father, and ironically, Lincoln's relationship with his oldest son, Robert, was little better. No doubt Abe's alienation from his father and son was due to his compassion and historical observations. Tom Lincoln was "sot" in his ways, and as an adult Robert was a conservative with little regard for the deprived. As many a wit described Robert Todd Lincoln, he was all Todd and no Lincoln.

Abe had an alert, creative outlook and was constantly studying and experimenting with all sorts of mechanical contraptions and social phenomena. He was a problem solver and experienced genuine distress at existing social evils like slavery. Furthermore, any conscientious youth worth his salt would want to rectify these inequities. Abe admired and supported this youthful enterprise as expressed in the following quotation:

"He (youth) has a great passion—a perfect rage-for the 'new'…. His horror is for all that is old, particularly 'Old Fogy'; and if there be any thing old which he can endure, it is only old whiskey and old tobacco."

WHEN WILL I JOIN A CHURCH?

No bona fide evidence exists proving that Lincoln ever joined a church. He loathed all of the emotionalism and fierce sectarian disputes that characterized organized religion in his day.

Supposedly, he made the following statement justifying his reluctance to join a denomination:

"When any church will inscribe over its altars, as its sole qualification for membership, the Savior's condensed statement for the substance of both law and gospel, 'Thou shalt love the Lord thy God with all thy heart, and with all thy soul, and all thy mind, and thy neighbor as thyself,' that church will I join with all my heart and soul." This statement has not been successfully proved by historians.

GRANT WAS RIGHT

On July 4, 1863, Vicksburg, Mississippi fell to the Union forces under the command of Ulysses Grant. Abe had not agreed with Grant's plan of attack and had written such. With characteristic frankness rarely displayed by presidents he wrote the following to his winning general:

"...I never had faith, except a general hope that you knew better than I, that the Yazoo Pass expedition and the like could succeed...I now wish to make the personal acknowledgement that you were right and I was wrong. A. Lincoln."

BENDING THE CONSTITUION TO SAVE IT

Because the nation had never experienced Civil War, Lincoln felt compelled to take unprecedented actions in order to save the union. Without the sanction of the law and/or the approval of the Congress, Abe issued a call for 300,000 volunteers for the US Army, ordered government funds to be given to persons he trusted to equip that army, revoked the Writ of Habeas Corpus and got the country in a war. This led to charges that he was breaking the law and ignoring the Constitution. Supreme Court Chief Justice, Roger Taney, lectured Abe about arresting persons and denying them of the Writ of Habeas Corpus. Abe responded, "Are all the laws, but one to go unexecuted, and the government itself go to pieces, lest that one be violated?"

Some of his actions were later ruled unconstitutional by the courts; others were upheld. Since most of these rulings were made after the Civil War, their results were of little consequence. Abe's major purpose—saving the union—had been accomplished, and most of the citizens of this nation have agreed with the outcome.

Being intellectually honest and apprising the public of the lack of law and precedent for his actions, Lincoln acknowledged:

"Yes,..(but)...was it possible to lose the nation, and yet preserve the Constitution? By general law life and limb must be protected, yet often a limb must be amputated to save a life; but a life is never wisely given to save a limb."

Many of Abe's unprecedented actions were adopted by later presidents. However, his informing the public of breaking the law and his reasons for doing so is a horse of another color.

FROM WHITE TO BLACK MOSES

Even before Abe's martyrdom, he was installed as "the father image" of the Negroes. As Black historian Benjamin Quarels wrote, "It is a matter of historical record that ...(the Negroes)... loved him first and have loved him longest."

With the influence of revisionist black writers and the dynamism of Martin Luther King this love of the white Father Abraham -–the white Moses —has lessened in recent times. Martin Luther King's, "I Have A Dream" speech delivered at the Lincoln Memorial became the "Second Emancipation Proclamation," and with his assassination in 1968, he became the Black Moses.

Peterson, 348-57.

GOATS IN THE WHITE HOUSE

One day Abe was entertaining a delegation of ladies in his office when a loud, thumping noise was heard coming from the hallway. Much to the amazement of the women, Tad drove past the open doorway with his pet goats harnessed in tandem to a chair.

As usual, Lincoln completely ignored this display by his youngest son as if nothing had happened and continued talking with the ladies. The ladies reacted quite differently. Just think: Goats in the White House!

MAKING THINGS GIT

G rant was such a pleasant and enjoyable experience for Abe. "I don't know what to make of Grant, he's such a quiet little fellow," said Lincoln, whose experience had been mainly with generals who let their presence be known to the eye and ear. "The only way I know he's around is by the way he makes things git!"

ABE'S ON OUR SIDE

Having written and spoken about so many topics, Abe, like the *Bible,* has been quoted to support a wide variety of opinions, positions and institutions. His words have been used by his opponents and supporters to prove that he was a racist, a socialist, a capitalist, a fundamental Christian, a spiritualist, a deist, an atheist, an advocate of interracial marriage, a prohibitionist, a promoter of hard liquor sales, et al. Ironically, the same statement or phrase has been used sometimes to support diametrically opposing groups. It could be enough to prompt Old Abe to say, "I'm not a Lincolnist."

Donovan, 76; Peterson, 340–62; and throughout the book.

MRS BIXBY'S LETTER

Dear Madam —

I have been shown in the files of the War Department a statement of the Adjutant General of Massachusetts that you are the mother of five sons who have died gloriously on the field of battle.

I feel how weak and fruitless must be any words of mine which should attempt to beguile you from the grief of a loss so overwhelming. But I cannot refrain from tendering to you the consolation that may be found in the thanks of the Republic they died to save.

I pray that our Heavenly Father may assuage the anguish of your bereavement, and leave you only the cherished memory of the loved and lost, and the solemn pride that must by yours, to have laid so costly a sacrifice upon the altar of freedom.

Yours, very sincerely and respectfully,

A. Lincoln —

In October of '64, Abe received information, verified by the War Department and the Adjutant General of Massachusetts, that Mrs. Bixby, a widow living in Boston, had lost all five of her sons preserving the Union. He could have written a letter to her and released it for campaign purposes before the election, but he didn't. After being re-elected, on November 21st, he sent through the War Department his letter to her which was personally delivered on Thanksgiving Day by Massachusetts Adjutant General Schouler. Without Lincoln's knowledge, Schouler made a copy of it and gave it to the newspapers.

Later it was revealed that only two of her sons died, but at the time, both Mrs. Bixby and the War Department genuinely believed them dead.

The letter was an instant success. As Sandburg so beautifully put it, "...the response to the Bixby letter, the love of its words...lay in the fact that in so many thousands of homes they did love the Union: they did hate slavery;(and they knew)...that human freedom so often was paid for with agony." SEE LETTERS

PARDONING A TURKEY

The death of Willie Lincoln had a devastating effect on the Lincolns. Sweet, sensitive and introspective, the boy was more like his father than any of the other children. Mary was incapacitated with grief, withdrew to her bedroom for an inordinate period of mourning and may have undergone a temporary nervous breakdown. Lincoln expressed his grief differently, but even he frequently broke down and cried in public over Willie. A year and a half later at Gettysburg he was still in mourning. A black band encircled the crown of Abe's hat. . .

With Willie's passing Tad and Abe became inseparable. The lad spent so much time with his father at the War Department Office that he learned the Morse Code used on the telegraph. Many evenings the child fell asleep in his father's office as Abe toiled late into the night. When Lincoln retired, he carried the sleeping child to his bedroom and laid him on a cot or allowed Tad to sleep with him.

Many accused Lincoln of spoiling the child, but he ignored their comments. He just wanted his fourth son to be a happy little boy. A friend gave Abe a large tom turkey for his Christmas dinner, but Tad made it a pet and named him Turkey Jack. When the boy learned that the turkey was headed for the dinner table, he begged and pleaded with his father not to surrender him to the cook and the chopping block, and Abe pardoned old Jack.

ABE'S COURT PACK

When Abe became President, a majority of the nine Supreme Court Justices were Southerners and Democrats. This proved to be a handicap to Lincoln as he endeavored to save the Union. Hoping to get a court that would approve of many of his actions and much of the new legislation passed by his Republican Congress, he had it enlarged to 10. With that seat and the retirement or death of justices, the Court eventually became a Lincoln court. Following the Civil War, when the tenth seat became vacant, the Court returned to the customary nine members.

Like Lincoln, Franklin Roosevelt, at the onset of his second term, tried to enlarge the Court to save important elements of his New Deal but was shot down by a hostile Congress. Although FDR has been considered one of the most politically astute presidents we have ever had, he failed where Abe suceeded.

UNWELCOMED GUESTS IN MEXICO

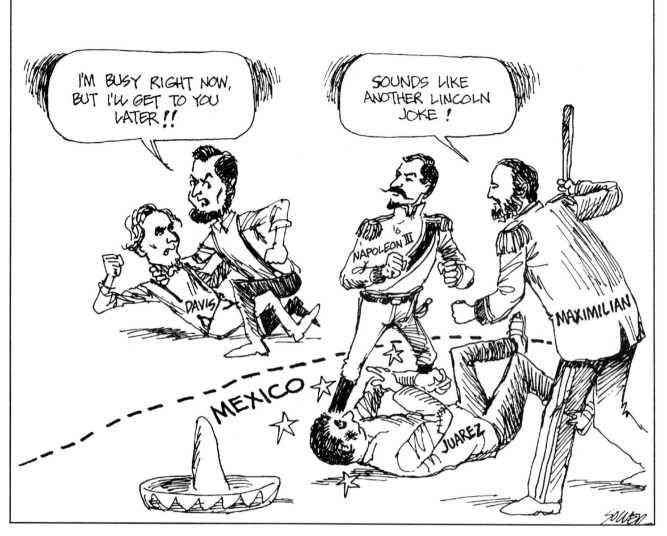

When Napoleon III sent in French troops and established a government under Maximilian, our nation was deeply involved in the Civil War. While his action was a definite violation of the Monroe Doctrine, there was little that Lincoln could do about it.

When queried about this situation, Abe made the following answer: "I'm not exactly 'skeered,' but I don't like the looks of the thing. Napoleon has taken advantage of our weakness in our time of trouble, and has attempted to found a monarchy on the soil of Mexico in utter disregard of the Monroe doctrine. My policy is, attend to only one trouble at a time. If we get well out of our present difficulties and restore the Union, I propose to notify Louis Napoleon that it is about time to take his army out of Mexico. When that army is gone, the Mexicans will take care of Maximilian."

As soon as Lee surrendered at Appomattox thirty Negro regiments from the old all black XXV Corps were sent to Texas to discourage the French. The action prompted the French to get out of Mexico, and Maximilian lost to the Mexicans and was executed.

NO JOKING, MR. PRESIDENT

Lincoln's humor came from many sources. Among them were his father, his experiences on the circuit as a lawyer, joke books, newspaper writers and *Aesop's Fables*.

As he matured and honed his repertoire of material, his purposes for telling his stories changed. Quoting Peterson's *Lincoln in American Memory*, "The stream of droll humor coexisted with Lincoln's life, changing as his life changed. In youth,... he told stories for the fun of it,...(as a lawyer), he employed wit and anecdote as tools of the trade, in politics as weapons of satire, and in the presidency as a kind of therapy..."

Moving into the White House did not change the habits of a lifetime of being a racontuer. He continued to tell his stories, which frequently were misunderstood by political and business interests and got him into trouble. His opponents are forgotten, but the stories are remembered and endear him to the world. He acknowledged the story in the cartoon as the best which described his predicament.

A TRUCE FOR THE LOVE OF MUSIC

Never has there been a war with such incongruities. Brutality was frequently tempered with sweet, tender acts of consideration and kindness for the enemy rarely exhibited in warfare. Often, hostilities ceased so that both sides could bury their dead, celebrate a religious service, observe a holiday or listen to a beautifully played song.

During the siege of Atlanta in August of '64, a temporary truce was held every evening so that both sides could enjoy a concert. A Georgia sharp shooter put aside his rifle, picked up his cornet and beautifully played a solo concert of songs both sides loved and knew, like "I Dreamt I Dwelt in Marble Halls" and "Come Where My Love Lies Dreaming."

How it got started or why the armies participated in these interludes is unknown, but, as irrational as war is, both sides lay down their weapons and listened to his wonderful music. They dreamed of home and loved ones and prayed for the long, cruel war to end. When the music ended, the war resumed as barbarically as before.

PLEASE, NOT THE RAILROAD CAR AGAIN!

One of the most popular myths regarding the 16th President concerns when the Gettysburg Address was written. Tradition renders its composition as an after thought hurriedly jotted down by Lincoln en route to Gettysburg. To anyone who knows Lincoln or politics the story is an exercise in fantasy. Successful politicians don't work that way.

Abe readily accepted the invitation to make a few appropriate remarks at the dedication of the military cemetery in early November of '63, because he knew that a large crowd would be there to hear Edward Everett, America's greatest living orator. Attending the ceremony would provide him with a golden opportunity to restate the war's aims and to do a little political fence mending. Being a slow and diligent writer, he immediately started drafting his remarks.

He guessed right, and the world had its first exposure to the most beloved and well known speech of all time, The Gettysburg Address.

THE DE-EMANCIPATION PROCLAMATION

On New Year's Day, 1863, Abe Lincoln signed the Emancipation Proclamation declaring that "henceforth all slaves in the states now in rebellion are now and forever free." The blacks, abolitionists and reformers quickly gave their approval. Before long the North as a whole also accepted the proposal.

However, south of the Mason and Dixon Line, it was greeted with scorn, ridicule and a shocking counter proclamation. On January 5, 1863, Jeff Davis responded in kind proclaiming that as of February 22, 1863, "all free Negroes in the Southern Confederacy shall be placed on the slave status, and deemed to be chattels, they and their issue forever. Furthermore, all Negroes captured in states where slavery did not exist would acquire the status of slaves."

TOO MANY BULLETS

Many of the Union generals were opposed to the adoption of cartridge firing rifles, because they feared the men would shoot too many bullets. Abe had considerable trouble getting the adoption of breach loaders which enabled Union soldiers to shoot four or five times faster than the old muzzle loaders. Having such rifles would give the troops a great advantage over the enemy.

Although we are inclined to scoff at the position taken by those officers, supply is always a problem for any army. But if life is valued and winning is important, such a reason is ridiculous and demoralizing to the men.

CAN THESE BE GODLY MEN?

When the leaders of the American Baptists' Association wrote a letter supporting the Union and Lincoln's Emancipation Proclamation, Abe wrote back thanking them for their help. He then castigated Southern ministers who had jointly attacked him and had appealed to the Christian nations of the world to come to the aid of the Confederacy.

"When...those professedly holy men of the South, met in the semblance of prayer and devotion, and, in the name of Him who said 'As ye would all men should do unto you, do ye even so unto them' appealed to the Christian world to aid them in doing to a whole race of men, as they would have no man do unto themselves, to my thinking, they contemned and insulted God and His church, far more than did Satan when he tempted the Saviour with the Kingdoms of the earth. The devil's attempt was no more false, and far less hypocritical...."

ABE'S FIB AT GETTYSBURG

Reluctant to use superlatives, it is Charlie B's contention that the Gettysburg Address is the most popular piece of prose ever composed by man. No doubt many religious and political organizations will disagree and will readily present their favorites such as the Sermon on the Mount, The Beatitudes, the Ten Commandments, et. al. However, these favorites are cherished by and unique to a small minority of the world's population. The Gettysburg Address is not subjected to such restraints and appeals to almost all peoples and philosophical persuasions. It is immune to the metes and bounds of religious doctrine.

In spite of its beauty and universal appeal, Abe did tell a fib at Gettysburg. You disagree? Well, consider this direct quote, "The world will little note nor long remember what we say here..." Need I say more?

ON BOTH SIDES

During the Civil War, conflicts developed regarding the matters of loyalty to the Union and freedom of religion and speech. An influential St. Louis minister, Dr. McPheeters, had been a problem to the Military Governor of the Department of Missouri, Major General Curtis. The preacher had made disloyal comments from the pulpit, and his church had been closed by the army. When Lincoln learned of the fracas, he wrote letters to the General regarding this delicate matter and rescinded Curtis' actions.

The minister was later tried by the general assembly of the Presbyterian Church for disloyalty, and parts of Abe's letters to Curtis were quoted by both sides to prove that the president was on their side. "So, it seems, Mr. President," reported Judge Jesse L. Williams of Indiana, "that it is not easy to tell where you stand."

Abe laughed and told the story of an Illinois farmer and his son who were out in the woods looking for a run-a-way sow. After a long search, they came to a creek branch where they found hog tracks and snout rootings, first on one side and then the other as they followed the stream's course. Finally, the father told his son, "Now, Bill, you take up on this side of the branch and I'll go up t'other, for I believe that old sow's on both sides of the crick."

DON'T CHANGE HORSES IN THE MIDDLE OF THE STREAM!

In 1864, Lincoln ran on the National Union Ticket and not as a Republican. His Vice Presidential running mate was Andrew Johnson, a Democrat from Tennessee. The Union Party's platform could be summed up in two words: Union and Abolition. Its slogan: Don't Change Horses in the Middle of the Stream.

General George McClellan was the Democratic standard bearer, and he campaigned on the issues of saving the Union and Slavery. The main point of disagreement between the major candidates was whether to retain or abolish slavery.

Oates, 430-31.

NO QUARTER ON BLACK TROOPS

There is very little that was civil in the Civil War. It was the bloodiest war this country has ever fought. Time and the media have romanticized the event and blunted its brutality and horrors. Ironically, the worst atrocities of that war have rarely mentioned the degree of brutality initially committed by southern troops against union black units and the retaliations by those black forces against their former masters. Also overlooked has been the sacrifice and commitment made by the white officers who commanded those Union black units. These black-white confrontations were the most ruthless and brutal incidents of the Civil War resulting in NO QUARTER massacres.

Prior to the Emancipation Proclamation (1/1/63), blacks were surreptitiously recruited, trained and experienced combat. According to the Lincoln Administration, they did not exist. After that date, official policy changed. Slaves were publicly encouraged to flee their masters and enlist. The servant grapevine broadcast freedom and encouraged black men to run away. They could fight for their freedom and help Old Abe save the Union, and thousands of them did. The majority of all enlistments after the implementation of the draft in July of '63, were blacks.

BLACK NO QUARTER ON REBEL TROOPS

JENKINS FERRY, ARK. AND PETERSBURG VIRGINIA MASSACRES

This Union practice was economically and militarily harmful to the Southern government, and it retaliated by declaring that black units and their white officers would be treated as criminals and not as prisoners of war. Field commanders could interpret this policy. Vanquished black and white outfits were subjected to NO QUARTER. Upon surrender hundreds of these soldiers were massacred at Ft. Pillow, Tennessee, Poison Springs, Arkansas, and Plymouth, North Carolina.

Lincoln tried to stop it with no effect, and Union generals informed their black units that they were on their own. As a result, Negro units responded in kind at Jenkins Ferry, Arkansas, Petersburg, Virginia, and elsewhere. Toward the end of the war rebel units became reluctant to engage them, which encouraged Union generals to have black units perform rear guard duty.

The Confederate policy backfired, for the lure of freedom was stronger than the fear of death, and blacks became ferocious fighters and intensely loyal to each other. For the remainder of the war, these units went into battle not expecting to raise or to honor a white flag. As Cornish states, "Negro soldiers and their (white) officers were bound together in a heightened esprit de corps and in a determination to die before surrendering that is rare in military annals."

CAVALRY HELL

With Willie Lincoln's passing Abe and his youngest son, Tad, became the closest of chums. The boy went with him most everywhere. Tad was born with a cleft palate and had a serious speech impediment. When he said "pappy day," it meant "papa dear," and few people understood him except the members of the family. Very energetic, a wiggler and active, he was impossible to teach. Tutors came and went, and it didn't bother his father. Tad had free run of the White House premises and did what he wanted.

He enjoyed strutting along with Captain Bennett while he inspected the cavalry on White House guard duty. One morning the captain saw that the men were getting lax and proceeded to bawl them out. "Men, the condition of quarters is disgraceful," he railed. "Instead of being kept like a US. Army Cavalry Unit, they look like_____" and while he hesitated Tad chirped, "hell!" For the rest of the day discipline was not so good.

DIGGIN' FOR THE KING OF SPADES

The Civil War did bring about many innovations in war tactics. When camped or on defense, Confederate General Longstreet ordered his soldiers to protect themselves by digging holes in the ground—the predecessor of WWII foxholes.

It was a great saver of lives, and General Lee, upon becoming commander of the Army of Northern Virginia, adopted the practice. He was such a stickler on this matter that his troops, behind his back, called him the King of Spades. They hated the digging, but his soldiers knew that he was right.

PICK ON ME; NOT MY WIFE

Abe Lincoln's popularity reached its lowest point in 1863. The politically astute were certain that he was a one-term president and would not get the Republican nomination in '64. Criticism came from every direction, including Republicans. Not only Abe, but those near him, including his wife, were targets.

Many of the snide attacks against Mary were personal. Her temperament and southern back-ground invited some of this criticism as well as being the most conspicuous female occupant of the White House since Dolly Madison. Because most of her family in Kentucky supported the South, Mary was accused of being a rebel spy. It was well known that three of her brothers and a brother–in–law died fighting for the Confederacy. This criticism became so intense that during the winter of 1862-63, a SECRET HEARING was called by the Senate Committee on the Conduct of the War. Abe got wind of the meeting. Uninvited and unannounced, he attended the meeting to defend his wife. His unexpected appearance caught them off guard. After a lengthy silence, he said, "I, Abraham Lincoln, President of the United States, appear of my own volition before this Committee of the Senate to say that I, of my own knowledge, know that it is untrue that any of my family hold treasonable communications with the enemy," and walked out. The astonished members adjourned without further discussion. The meeting was a part of a larger scheme being plotted at the time to impeach Lincoln.

A FRENCH TRICK

During Lincoln's first administration, by an act of Congress, Gallaudet University was founded to teach the deaf and blind. Abe Lincoln signed its charter, and Edward Miner Gallaudet became its first leader. Later, Gallaudet stopped teaching the blind, and today it is the most outstanding university in the world for the deaf.

Rumor circulates among the deaf that Abe's hands on French's statue at the Lincoln Memorial are signing the letters A and L. Artists have been known to subtly include special messages and have occasionally played tricks on their patrons. Did French include a special message?

If possible, next time you visit the Memorial, take a deaf person with you to verify the rumor. Ask a deaf friend or relative what they think. That is how I was made aware of it. Most deaf persons have a special affection for Old Abe, and the reason given for their love of the man is because of his involvement with the founding of Gallaudet University.

I NEED SOMEBODY

In late 1861, the Congress created a watch dog body, the Committee on the Conduct of the War. At times it did help Abe, but frequently it was a gad fly and pain in the neck to him. Its chairman was the liberal Republican Senator from Ohio, Benjamin Franklin Wade. He was always after Abe about the conduct of the war.

One day he strode into the White House and stormily told the President to fire McClellan. Abe asked him who he should put in McClellan's place? To which Wade snorted, "Anybody!" Lincoln cooly replied, "Wade, anybody will do for you, but I must have somebody."

TOO OLD TO CRY

The fall elections of '62 roughed up the Republicans and Lincoln, resulting in the Democrats doubling their number in the Congress. The voters were most upset at the failures of Abe's Generals and the staggering numbers of dead and wounded. Also, Abe's preliminary Emancipation Proclamation of late September '62 was not well received. The Republican administration got waxed.

When the final returns came in, Lincoln was asked how he felt about it. He responded in typical fashion by telling the story of the young man who stumped his toe while running to meet his sweetheart and fell to the ground with bone shaking force. Jumping up, bouncing around on his good foot while holding his big toe and in great pain, the young man said he was too old to cry, and it hurt too much to laugh.

Oates, 350; War Years, 216.

THE OTHER SIDE OF THE TOO BIG TO CRY

The "too big to cry" story is known and retold many times. However, there is another side of the story that is not well known but has a very good point.

As Abe and a companion walked home through the wet, gloomy streets of Springfield on the night of Douglas' victory in 1858, his feet slipped and he almost fell. Lincoln recovered, and he said to his friend as they continued walking,

"My foot slipped from under me, knocking the other out of the way; but I recovered and said to myself, 'It's a slip and not a fall.'"

WHAT KIND OF RELIGION, LADIES?

The first Thursday of December of '64, two ladies from Tennessee appealed to President Lincoln to free their Confederate husbands from a Union prisoner of war camp upon the grounds that the husbands should be free because they were religious persons. He put them off until the next day, and then told them to come back the next day, Saturday. He then ordered the release of the prisoners, and said the following to the wives:

"You say that your husband is a religious man; tell him when you meet him, that I am not much of a judge of religion, but that, in my opinion, the religion that sets men to rebel and fight against their government, because, as they think, that government does not sufficiently help some men to eat their bread on the sweat of other men's faces, is not the sort of religion upon which people can get to heaven!"

FIVE FEET FOUR WILL DO IN A PINCH

Most of the successful Civil War Generals—Blue or Gray—were the objects of great dedication and affection from their men. They exposed themselves to the same murderous fire their soldiers experienced, and many of them were wounded and killed in action. For example, at the Battle of Nashville near the end of the war six Confederate generals were killed.

Phil Sheridan, a short (5'4") Irish graduate of West Point, was greatly admired by his men. One day in late '63, while they waited for orders to advance against rebel gunners occupying the heights at Lookout Mountain, Sheridan raised his flask and toasted the enemy. They returned his gentlemanly gesture with cannon fire, nearly hitting him. That act so enraged Sheridan's men that, without a word being said, they charged up the mountain and overwhelmed the enemy.

When General Grant asked, "Who ordered those men to charge?" an aide volunteered, "No one, Sir. When those fellows get started, all hell can't stop them."

In the late summer of '64, Sheridan was directed by Grant to run Jubal Early's Confederate force out of the Shenandoah Valley. There were many Southern sympathizers in the region, and in order to accomplish the task he burned and destroyed anything of value within the area. According to his troops, food was so scarce that a rabbit had to carry a meal to get across the valley.

Abe was so elated at Sheridan's accomplishment that he told the fiery little Irishman, "When this particular war began, I thought a cavalryman should be at least six feet four inches high, but I have changed my mind. Five feet four will do in a pinch."

Oates, 428-432; Burns, 260-61.

NOT A MILE FROM HELL!

In the minds of his countrymen, good old George Washington was the Father of His Country before his death. Loved and respected by all, he unhappily discovered that by the constitutional structure of our government, the President and the Congress can never be friends. Even in the best of times, the relationship is uneasy. As an honorable man and our least political president, Washington was hurt by that discovery.

Abe's disposition and outlook were quite different. As a politician, he understood the value and functions derived from the separation of powers of the government and the roles that must be played by the parties involved. Abe dismissed this necessary contention with humor as a part of the democratic process.

One day, Ohio Senator, Ben Wade, came charging into Lincoln's office demanding that he fire Grant. With his cool, unflappable manner he said, "Have a seat, Senator, and, by the way that reminds me of a story."

"That's the way it is with you, Sir," retorted Wade, "all story, stories. You are the Father of every military blunder that has ever been made in this war. You are on the road to Hell, Sir, with the government, by your obstinacy. Why, you're not a mile from there this very moment."

Looking up with a sly wink Abe asked, "Senator, isn't that just about the distance from here to the Capital?"

COMPASSION FOR ALEC

In matters not political, Abe was most kind and considerate, even to political opponents and rebel leaders. After the failed peace conference at Hampton Roads in early 1865, Lincoln asked his old friend and Whig ally of the Thirtieth Congress, Confederate Vice President Alexander Stephens, if there was anything of a personal nature that he could do for him. Alec first said nothing and then asked Lincoln if he could send his nephew home from the Union prison at Johnson's Island. Abe replied that he would be glad to, and he did.

UNCLE BILLIE'S SPARE TUNNEL COMMITTEE

In April of '64, Sherman launched Lincoln's long awaited campaign to take Atlanta, Georgia, the South's second largest industrial city and its major railhead. He was probably the most brilliant, creative general of the war and the originator of the concept of total warfare. His adversary was one of the Confederacy's best, Joe Johnston.

"Uncle Billie," as his troops affectionately called him, knew that attacking Johnston's dug-in troops was deadly and avoided it. He divided his forces into three armies led by trusted and competent generals. While one army feigned attacking Joe Johnston's defending troops frontally, the other two circled to the right and left in flanking movements toward Atlanta. In order to defend the city from the flanking armies, Johnston had to abandon his position and retreat to a new location to head them off, whereby the center

made an advance without an engagement. This scenario was replayed many times with the same results. One can empathize with the rebel troopers who said, "We know Uncle Billie Sherman ain't a go'in to Hell, 'cause he'll outflank the Devil all the way to Heaven." By this method Sherman almost reached Atlanta before losing his patience and engaging Johnston at Kennesaw Mountain and amassing huge Union losses. He never did that again, and rather than attack defending southern forces at Atlanta, he surrounded the city and starved them into submission.

His engineers were brilliant and rebuilt railroad trestles and tunnels faster than Nathan Bedford Forrest could blow them up. A Confederate private frustratingly opined, "Billie Sherman's got everything. Why he even travels with a spare tunnel."

Burns, 322,323.

WHERE'S SHERMAN?

On November 15th, 1864, General William Sherman launched the most audacious military campaign in modern history. His 60,000 strong army completely disappeared in enemy country for 32 days with no communication to the outside world. It lived off the land and deliberately left a sixty mile wide swath of destruction in Georgia from Atlanta to the sea.

Sherman's lengthy silence aroused the fears of his army's loved ones. Feeding this fear were untrue articles printed by Southern editors and recirculated in northern newspapers depicting the deplorable and demoralized plight of his army. Politicians and the people again questioned Lincoln's judgment and demanded that he act. Abe consulted General Grant, who assured him that Sherman's army was in little danger and that when "Uncle Billie" decided to come out, he would. Abe then responded to an anxious public: "General Grant assures me, that Sherman's army is safe with such a general, and, like a gopher, if he can't get out where he want's to, he can crawl back by the hole he went in at." News of Savannah's fall on December 21,, delighted Lincoln and the people, and the world was amazed at Uncle Billie's genius."

BENEFITS FOR UNWED MOTHERS WITH CHILDREN

The acrimonious debate regarding the expenditure of federal aid for unwed mothers with children originated during the Civil War. It arose in the debates over the benefits and payments given to black soldiers following the Emancipation Proclamation. Initially, these benefits were for the dependents of white soldiers who were legally married. Under slavery, state law decreed that marriage did not exist for slaves and that their children were illegitimate. Since almost all of the black soldiers had been slaves, would their wives and children be denied the benefits given to whites? Immediately a moral argument broke out, and the Congress refused to give such benefits to unwed black men, their wives and children.

Under the leadership of liberal Republicans like Senator Charles Sumner, similar benefits were granted to black dependents during the summer of 1864. Lincoln supported Sumner and others in attaining those benefits as the excerpt from the following letter attests: "Widows and children in fact, of colored soldiers who fall in our service,(must) be placed in law; the same as if their marriages were legal, so that they can have the benefits of the provisions made the widows and orphans of white soldiers." Dare we call this aid to unwed mothers with children?

A GLORIOUS OCCASION: NEW YEAR'S DAY, '65

As was the custom for New Year's Day, the White House held a reception for Congressmen, Cabinet members, foreign dignitaries and some members of the public on January 1, 1865. It was the fourth such occasion for the Lincolns, and they greeted guests with Abe shaking their hands for over two hours.

Outside, among the onlookers, was a large group of Blacks. Some were wearing fine clothes; others wore pickings from rag bags. Finally, they decided to enter the White House and see their hero, President Lincoln. When he saw them at the door, Abe welcomed the motley crowd, and for the first time the front door of the White House received black folks. They laughed and cried and cried and laughed as they shook his hands and exclaimed through blinding tears: "God Bless you!" "God Bless Ab-raham Lincoln!" "God Bress Marse Linkum!"

CHAPLAINS FOR ALL

Abe was tolerant of all faiths and had no patience for the expression of sectarian views, prejudices or stereotypes involving military life. When certain commanders issued orders which discriminated against members of different faiths, he interceded and appointed Catholic priests and Jewish rabbis chaplains. When a delegation of Negro Baptist ministers became concerned about the spiritual life of black soldiers, Abe listened to their concerns and wrote a blanket directive to military officials asking that Negro clergymen be afforded facilities "which may not be inconsistent with or a hindrance to military operations."

This attitude was expressed in matters not spiritual. Lincoln revoked Grant's Order No. 11 prohibiting Jews as a class from trading with the Army of Tennessee. The general did have a problem with corruption and price gouging of his troops and took action to stop it, but his solution was unfair and discriminatory. Fearful that the Sisters of Charity at Bardstown, Kentucky, might have their property confiscated by the Union Army, Abe telegraphed a protective order. Although the military hospitals of the Sisters of Mercy in Chicago and Washington were privately owned, he instructed the War Department to provide them with free supplies. Also, he returned the lands to the California Missions during his tenure.

War Years, 176, 633, 783; Peterson, 230-232; Quarles, 253.

AN HUMBLE PRESIDENT

Abe rarely allowed slights or acts of rudeness by persons to control his judgement in professional and political situations. He was far more concerned with results, what was best for the country, and the occasion or the people involved. He did not carry grudges as displayed by his relationships with Stanton and McClellan.

As chief counsel in the McCormack Case, Edwin Stanton had been very rude and inconsiderate to Lincoln. Originally, Abe was hired as co-counsel when the case was to be tried in Illinois. When a change of venue to Ohio was granted, Stanton completely ignored "that country hick lawyer from Illinois." Years later, Lincoln appointed him Secretary of War, because Stanton was a very capable, effective administrator who got the War Department on the ball. In time Stanton came to admire Lincoln and was one of his strongest cabinet supporters. Initially, like so many of us, he mistook style for substance.

Lincoln's patience with the arrogance and disrespect displayed toward him by General McClellan produced the story of his willingness to hold the general's horse if Little Mac would bring him victories. It's a good story, but there is little proof to substantiate it.

WHOSE BOOTS DO THEY BLACK

While most of Lincoln's humor was spontaneous and clever, sometime it could be satirical. Frequently it was used to prick the pretentious, to barb the arrogant and aloof. Various versions told by different persons have circulated about the following incident:

One day Abe was blacking his boots when Secretary of Treasure Chase walked into his office unannounced. Surprised at seeing the President doing such an humble task, Chase asked,

"Why Mr. President, you black your own boots?

"Yes, " replied Abe.

"But Mr. President, gentlemen don't black their boots," continued Chase.

"Whose boots do they black, Mr. Secretary?"

TO BEARD OR NOT TO BEARD

As Abe prepared for a very close race in his bid for re-election in early 1864, he seriously considered cutting off his beard. Lincoln had grown his beard after he had been elected in '60, and many persons had criticized him for breaking with the tradition. He was very unpopular at the time and wondered if shaving off the beard might help his chances.

It was so important that Lincoln ordered the Osborne Coinage Company of Cincinnati, Ohio, to prepare two sets of dies for the campaign coin his party would give away to voters as gifts in the election. Abe finally decided to keep his beard. Would he have lost by shaving it off? Did Old Abe win in '64 by the hair on his chinny chin chin? Imagine what a "close shave" would have done to the penny, the five dollar bill, French's statue at the Lincoln Memorial and all those pictures seen in post offices, school houses and public buildings. Would people have faith in those cities, insurance companies, banks, and other businesses that rely on the Lincoln name as a merchandising tool with Abe sans beard?

AN UPSIDE DOWN UNDERGROUND RAILROAD.

Throughout the war, southern masters circulated fabricated horror stories about yankee atrocities committed on slaves. This was done in hopes of stopping runaways and to dissuade blacks from helping escaping union soldiers, but it met with little success. The slaves knew better. Little happened throughout the war that they did not find out about through the "grapevine." Instead of fearing the yankee soldiers they fed, clothed and helped them evade authorities on their way north.

"The Negroes of the South had a great deal of surreptitious knowledge, and her bondsmen were a conclave of unrecognized free masons," wrote James Guthrie. Yankee prisoners of war were not afraid to hit the slave shacks for food, clothing and guides in assisting their escape from rebel prisons. The blacks' familiarity with the operations of the underground railroad had given them valuable experience in the techniques of flight and concealment. The underground railroad was turned upside down.

Quarles, 46-53, 79, 267-272.

ABE'S GHOST WRITER

By tradition and practice in Lincoln's day, many successful professional men served as mentors, helping young men learn their professions. Young men read the law and clerked for practicing attorneys while learning the trade. Abe did the same with quite a few young men. One of them was John Hay, an Indiana youth who went to Springfield to study law with an uncle. He decided to leave the Illinois prairie and the law when Abe offered him a job as assistant secretary in Washington.

A graduate from Brown, Hay was in many ways like his boss, being an amateur poet and greatly interested in politics, drama and philology, (the study of words and their meanings). They spent many hours together discussing these subjects, and during that period John Hay learned to copy his boss's handwriting and signature. Certain kinds of letters were assigned by Lincoln for Hay to compose, sign and mail. Many think that the letter to Mrs. Bixby was actually copied by Hay.

GIVE'M A CHANCE

One day Abe met a robust young man in the streets and said, "You look like an able bodied man-why don't you join the army?" When the man answered that he'd be glad to die for his country if only given a chance, Abe wrote out the following note, gave it to him and directed the man to the local recruiter.

Col. Fielding

The bearer is anxious to go to the front and die for his country. Can't you give him a chance?

A Lincoln

IT'LL NEVER WORK

The South had no navy at the beginning of the war, but under its creative Secretary of the Navy, Stephan Mallory, it began building a small fleet of iron ships. By the fall of '61, the southerners were converting the US steam frigate Merrimack into an ironclad.

When Union counterpart, Gideon Wells, expressed his deep concern about the project to top brass, they dismissed it as impractical and without merit. Not content, he encouraged John Ericsson to design an ironclad ship and presented his designs to navy brass who also rejected them . Still concerned, Wells went to Lincoln. Upon studying the designs, Abe responded, "Well, Mr. Secretary, like the young lady said when she put on her sock, 'I think there's something in it.' Go ahead and build the ship." Within 101 days Ericsson launched the strange little craft, the Monitor, and sent it on its way.

On March 8, 1862, the refitted Merrimack, departed Newport Harbor and quickly sank two of the US Navy's largest war ships and seriously damaged a third, the Minnesota, which was beached. Panic struck the north, and for a day the Confederate Navy ruled the world.

Fortunately for the Union, that night the Monitor arrived and moored itself to the stricken Minnesota. Early the next morning, when the Merrimack steamed out to destroy the wounded ship, it unexpectedly confronted the Monitor. During an eight hour battle, neither ship could inflict serious damage to the other. Low on supplies, the Merrimack retreated to Newport Harbor and was never used again. However, that battle made every wooden navy in the world obsolete.

USHER LINDER'S CHRISTMAS GIFT

In partisan politics, Abe could be unrelenting and at times ruthless. However, in things not political, issues of the heart and daily living, his humane and considerate behavior to his fellow creatures is well known, even extending to his political enemies.

In Charleston, Douglas Democrat and lawyer Usher F. Linder's son joined the Confederate Army and was taken prisoner. His father sent letters to Lincoln asking for a pardon. During Christmas of '63, Linder received the following note from his old Eighth Judicial Circuit acquaintence; "Your son Dan, has just left me, with my order to the Secretary of War, to administer to him the oath of allegiance, discharge him & send him to you."

IF ALL MEN WERE JUST, WE WOULD STILL NEED GOVERNMENT

Throughout our history there has been a lot of debate about the necessity of government and its purposes. Here is what Abe had to say about it:

"The legitimate object of government, is to do for a community of people, whatever they need to have done, but cannot do, at all, or cannot, so well do, for themselves in their separate, and individual capacities. In all that the people can individually do as well for themselves, government ought not to interfere. The desirable things which the individuals of a people cannot do, or cannot well do, for themselves, fall into two classes: those which have relation to wrongs, and those which have not. Each of these branch off into an infinite variety of subdivisions.

The first—that in relation to wrongs—embraces all crimes, misdemeanors, and non-performance of contracts. The other embraces all which, in its nature, and without wrong, requires combined action, as public roads and highways, public schools, charities, pauperism, orphanage, estates of the deceased, and the machinery of government itself. From this it appears that if all men were just, there still would be some, though not so much, need of government."

THAT 42 POUND BABY

Throughout most of the war Lincoln's generals continually overestimated the size of the Confederate forces they fought. It was constantly given as an excuse for not initiating action. Until they had more men and materials, they just could not engage him. Abe was quite certain his generals had superior forces and was disgusted at their dawdling. This tendency on their part reminded him of the Illinois fisherman at Alton, Illinois, who always overestimated the size of the fish he caught. It reached a point were his neighbors didn't believe him. In order to convince them that he was telling the truth he purchased a pair of scales. After that, every time he caught a big fish he weighed it while his friends watched, and they believed him.

This worked quite well until one evening a nearby lady had a baby. The attending doctor did not have his scales to weigh the newborn. Knowing that the nearby fisherman had scales at his house, the doctor had the father get them, and they weighed the infant. That baby weighed forty-two pounds!

WHO GAVE US THIS BRUTAL WAR?

*2ND INAUGURAL ADDRESS, MARCH 4, 1865

If any president were ever to go before the American people and state that the reason for their Civil War was an expression of the will of God visited upon them for past sins, he would be destroyed. Like poor Humpty Dumpty, all of the president's spin doctors and all of the president's Madison Avenue's PR men could not put that president back together again. He would be ostracized and forgotten by his country, and his words consigned to outer darkness. And yet, Abraham Lincoln actually did that in his Second Inaugural Addres—a speech that has been unanimously accepted as one of the greatest and most eloquent ever given. Rather than having these words censured and burned on bonfires, they have been chiseled in stone and in the hearts and minds of his fellow citizens. When we read or recite these words from memory, we seem to be oblivious to the import of the sentence which justifies the duration of the war as a price extracted by God. Let us re-read that sentence: "Yet, if God wills that it (Civil War) continue, until all the wealth piled by the bondman's two hundred and fifty years of un-requited toil shall be sunk, and until every drop of blood drawn with the lash, shall be paid by another drawn with the sword, as was said three thousand years ago, so still it must be said, 'the judgments of the Lord are true and righteous altogether.'" Did Abe actually mean that? Yes! In response to a letter from New York politician Thurlow Weed, complementing Lincoln on the speech, he wrote on March 15th: "Men are not flattered by being shown that there has been a difference of purpose between the Almighty and them. To deny it, however, in this case, is to deny that there is a God governing the world. It is a truth which I thought needed to be told;…"

TAKE SKIM MILK IF YOU CAN'T GET CREAM

During Salmon P. Chases's years as Abe's Secretary of the Treasure, he had been a constant source of trouble. The Ohioan had always felt that he should have been president and that Lincoln was not qualified for the job and had served poorly in that capacity. Abe had tolerated his political plotting and scheming for almost four years before finally accepting his resignation, because he was a very good Treasurer and a liberal Republican who sincerely desired freedom for the blacks.

Although Chase had been a thorn in his side, Lincoln appointed him Chief Justice of the Supreme Court, because he considered him to be the best man for the job. Chase was surprised with the appointment but accepted the position half heartedly. He could not bring himself to accept the sage political advice he had frequently given to others. "Be satisfied with skim milk when you can't get cream."

A FEW VICES AND A LOT OF VIRTUE

On the twin vices of whiskey and tobacco Abe once said, "I drank enough drams of whiskey to realize I didn't like its taste and it wasn't good for me, and I used enough tobacco to know that I didn't care for it, and it wasn't good for me either." Lincoln felt that whiskey left him flabby and undone, blurred his vision and threatened his control, so he avoided it.

Consistent with his belief that people had a right to make choices, he tolerated these vices. He didn't mind if others drank. Also, according to Sandburg and Donald, Abe ran a still for a while at New Salem, an art known and practiced by frontier farmers from colonial days. The Lincoln and Berry Store sold such products in New Salem, but hard spirits or tobacco were not for Abe.

UNCLE SAM'S U.S.C.T.

At times great truths are learned while visiting cemeteries. Ambling among the grave stones and markers of the First United States National Cemetery at Ft. Scott, Kansas, my brother and I made a revealing discovery about a particular group of men that had served our country honorably and well— a group whose accomplishments had been almost completely ignored and/or omitted from the history books.

A majority of the graves contained the remains of men who had died prior to the 20th Century, predominantly veterans of the Civil and Indian wars. The customary data found on such monuments—names, dates of birth and death, rank and state military units—were chiseled into the stone. Occasionally, we came upon a different type of tombstone. They were plain, rectangular Army monuments with a U.S. Shield carved near the outer edges of the stone. Within the shield was the name of the occupant, date of death and rank and one of the following series of letters: U.S.C.T., U.S. Col. Inf., or U.S. Col. Cav. Rarely was the date of birth given or any state mentioned. We were intrigued by these plain stones with their simple captions and desired to know more about them. At the cemetery's office we learned that they represented United States Colored Troops, Infantry or Cavalry.

Most of these men had been born in slavery, which explained the lack of the date of birth. They had fought for the United States Government and Old Abe Lincoln who had given them their freedom and the opportunity to prove that they were men. In a sense, their plain tombstones displayed their disdain for state's rights, which had given them slavery and the humiliation of being called boys. They were proud to be remembered as just plain U.S.C.T.'s.

Fort Scott National Cemetery bulletins; Cornish, 131; Quarles, 213.

`THE TEN CANNOT-MENTS

A by-product of the ever changing Lincoln legend is the production of misquotes and positions phrased in rail splitter rhetoric. Through popular usage they are accepted as authentic Lincoln though they never flowed from his pen or lips. A classic example of this practice is the ten "Lincoln Cannot–Ments."

Stated as fitting observations written by Lincoln more than a century ago, they proclaim his words of wisdom that still ring true today. Here are some of the "Cannot–Ments:"

"You cannot help small men by tearing down big men.

You cannot bring about prosperity by discouraging thrift.

You cannot help the poor man by destroying the rich."

Abe had nothing to do with them, and many speakers—even presidents—have quoted them as gospel Lincoln, unaware of their dubious origin. They are the offspring of minister William Boetcher and were first printed in 1916. In fairness to Reverend Boetcher, when he wrote those homilies, he put authentic Lincoln quotations on the reverse side of his text and never intended to produce a counterfeit.

WASTE THOSE CANNOT-MENTS, CHARLIE B

The Cannot-ments, like other mythical Lincoln material, make great political and philosophical oratory, but prudent speakers shun them. They check their Lincoln lines for their authenticity with respected scholars or organizations like the Illinois State Historical Library at Springfield, Illinois.

DUBIOUS ORIGINS

The impulsive responses of the impish, nimble mind of Lincoln have produced some of the greatest one-liners in history. One day an office seeker, desiring a presidential appointment, sought to impress Abe by writing in a letter that he was a direct descendant of colorful Congressman, John Randolph of Roanoke, Virginia. Not carefully checking his references, the man had a minor hitch in his pitch to the President. Apparently he was unaware that John Randolph was impotent and had never sired any children. Furthermore, this condition was well known by fellow Congressmen and had been the source of some of the most colorful, ribald remarks ever made on the floor of the House of Representatives. Being a former Congressman, Abe knew all about it.

Greatly amused at the gentleman's dubious genealogy, Abe gave him the appointment but could not resist writing on the back of his commission, "A direct decendent from one who was never a father."

KEEP THE CHAMPAGNE, BUT RETURN THE NEGRO!

On February 3, 1865, Lincoln and Secretary of State Seward met aboard a steamer off of Hampton Roads with three Confederate commissioners to discuss terms for a possible peace. Lincoln refused to yield on the twin demands of union and emancipation, and the discussions ended.

After the southerners had returned to their steamer, Seward decided to send some bottles of champagne to the commissioners, who were old friends. A rowboat with Seward's black servant at the oars took them the gift. As his old friends waved a goodbye and their thanks from their craft, Seward shouted through the boatswain's trumpet, "Keep the champagne, but return the Negro!" Thus ended the doomed Hampton Roads peace negotiations.

ABE'S TOWER OF BABEL

Lord Curzon, Chancellor of the University of Oxford, once stated that the three supreme masterpieces of English eloquence were the Toast of William Pitt (The Younger) after the defeat of the French Navy at Trafalgar and Abe Lincoln's Gettysburg and Second Inaugural addresses.

Heartily agreeing with such an imminent authority, we love these words and have chiseled them in stone at the Lincoln Memorial. so that everyone may view them and pay their respects to Old Abe.

Although citizens of the United States claim Lincoln and his words, the world has appropriated the man and his messages. When recited in the stilted English of admiring foreigners, "Four score and seven years ago" thrills us, gratifies them and immediately creates a bond of friendship.

ON FOOL'N THE PEOPLE

One of the all time great quotes credited to the Rail Splitter is the one about fool'n the people: "It is true that you can fool all of the people some of the time; you can even fool some of the people all of the time; but you can't fool all of the people all of the time."

There is no credible evidence that Abe ever said it, but, if he were alive today, he would probably respond to the quote as he did about General Grant's favorite brand of whiskey: "You will just have to charge it to me to give it currency."

MERRY SANTA ABE

By New Year's Day, 1865, Lincoln knew that the Civil War would soon be over, and he now sought to consummate a long cherished political goal—the adoption of the Thirteenth Amendment abolishing slavery. He deeply feared that Congress, the courts or a later president would overturn or revoke the Emancipation Proclamation. An amendment abolishing slavery would be, as he phrased it, "a King's cure for all the evils." He had tried to get the amendment proposed in early '64, and the Senate had approved it, only to have it rejected by the House.

Since he had been re-elected and the Congress was now in a "Lame duck" session, Abe again urged the House to approve it. There is no recorded evidence that Abe personally twisted arms and distributed the loaves and fishes of patronage to get reluctant House Democrats and Conservative Republicans to vote for the Thirteenth Amendment. However, his past history of being a master at dispensing such favors indicates to the contrary. Slavery had been the most abiding, controversial issue the nation had faced. The Emancipation Proclamation had nearly cost him re-election. To assume that he did not pull every lever and string he had access to ignores historical, political reality. Vitriolic old Thaddeus Stevens was correct when he remarked, "The greatest measure of the nineteenth century was passed by corruption and aided and abetted by the purest man in America."

And it came to pass that on January 31, 1865, the House of Representatives by two-thirds vote proposed the Thirteenth Amendment to abolish slavery. With its ratification the second controversial issue of Abe's adult life was solved by his generation.

LOVE IS ETERNAL

Despite their differences, the stormy, unhappy marriage of the Lincolns reported by many is not true. The same can be said about Abe being a battered husband. Modern historical research reveals, ..."their marriage was a good one; they were partners politically, and totally devoted to each other." The late '50's were wonderful times for the couple. Abe's practice provided ample income, they remodelled their little house on Eighth Street, and Mary was proud of the success of her husband as a lawyer and the leader of the Republicans.

Because of all the ways he cared for her, Lincoln was everything to Mary, "lover, husband, father, all." Certainly not the picture that Billy Herndon and many of Mary's other enemies proclaimed after Abe's death. Their love was eternal.

Peterson, 50; Oates, 72; Lincoln, 197.

LET THE LIGHT SHINE

On February 22, 1865, Lincoln ordered that the high-domed building on the top of Capitol Hill be illuminated at night, signifying Sherman's victories in South Carolina and that more area was coming again under the U.S. Flag. This observance continued with the announcement of other Union victories until the end of the Civil War.

THE SECRETARIES' HISTORY

When Abe left Springfield to go to Washington, he took with him a couple of bright, young men, John Nicolay and John Hay, to serve as his principal secretaries. He called them "the boys" and between themselves, they called him the "Ancient" and the "Tycoon." (As to what they called Mrs. Lincoln, the least said the better.) No other two men had a closer, day-to-day relationship with the Sixteenth President. From the first they idolized him, and he constantly grew in their esteem until, after his death, their worship was unbounded.

Early in the Lincoln administration they conceived the idea of a biography on Lincoln, which they published in the 1890's. Consisting of ten volumes, it did much to enshrine the Civil War President's memory and furthered the establishment of the Lincoln legend. Since very few read the complete works today, its fame did not last, and their volumes gather dust in many libraries.

WOULD YOU SHAKE MY HAND?

Lincoln never considered the Civil War one of southern independence; it was a rebellion that must be put down to save the Union. Few realize that the loss of life and limb was of such tragic proportions. Every man, regardless of the side he fought on, was ours, and the nation suffered the loss. Thus, from the beginning of the war, whenever Abe had the opportunity, he visited the wounded at the hospitals whether they were Union or Rebel soldiers. He genuinely expressed his concern and promised the best possible care for all of them. As a result, some of his most trenchant enemies admired him.

In early April of '65, Abe visited the wounded at the City Point, Virginia, hospitals. There were nearly 5,000 wounded from both armies, and he tried to shake hands with everyone of them.

In the Confederate tents he came upon Col. Harry L. Benbow, shot torn in both hips. As Lincoln extended his hand, Benbow said, "Mr. President, do you know to whom you offer your hand?" Benbow relates:

"I do not," he replied.

"Well," I said, "you offer it to a Confederate colonel who has fought you as hard as he could for four years."

"Well," he said, "I hope a Confederate colonel will not refuse me his hand."

"No, sir," I replied, "I will not, and I clasped his hand in both of mine."

FIGHT'N FOR THE VOTE

April 11, 1865, was a great day for the residents of Washington. News had circulated throughout the city the day before of Lee's surrender and that the Civil War was over. It seemed that the whole city was celebrating the victory. That night a great crowd assembled in front of the north portico of the White House to hear President Lincoln deliver an address. The crowd expected to hear a patriotic encomium of victory and jubilation. Instead he delivered a very serious speech regarding the reconstruction of the southern states recently at rebellion. This was not what the crowd wanted to hear. Little did the celebrants realize that it was to be his last address.

Though various reasons have been given as to why he gave such a speech, it has never been fully answered. Contained within the speech was an ancillary statement of great significance for the former slaves. For the first time in our history a president publicly announced that he was in favor of BLACKS VOTING. Abe said, "I would prefer that it(the vote) were now conferred on the very intelligent, and on those who serve our cause as soldiers." Near the close of his address he re-fortified his position on black suffrage by suggesting that this right should apply to all of the southern states that had rebelled.

JUDGMENTS BY JUDGE LYNCH

In a letter to General James Blunt dated August 18, 1863, Abe wrote,"Judge Lynch sometimes take(s) jurisdiction of cases which prove too strong for the courts." This position appears to be a hundred and eighty degree reversal from that taken by Lincoln in his Young Men's Lyceum Speech of '38. Then he had expressed deep concern about the recent rash of lynchings in the Mississippi River Valley, stating that there was no grievance that was a fit object of redress by mob law. Lincoln had always been a law and order man who had great faith in the system of justice to resolve the controversial issues affecting society.

What came over Abe? Why would he make such a statement a quarter of century later? Was it the Civil War? Or was it an honest observation of what frequently happens when the institutions of law enforcement fail to carry out their assigned mission? Recently a virtuous man felt compelled to shoot and kill a bully that had terrorized his Southern California community for over two years. Everyone in the neighborhood, including the elements of law enforcement knew of the offender's brutal behavior. Now the community's hero—a retired US Naval officer-—has been found guilty of manslaughter for taking the law into his hands. Is this an example of what Abe was writing about?

NO PARDON THIS TIME

Lincoln's compassion for men condemned to be executed is well known. However, at times he could be as hard as nails. Such was his treatment of Nathaniel Gordon of Maine, a slave trader caught on the high seas attempting to import blacks into the South during the Civil War. Some of Lincoln's best friends tried to get him to commute or pardon Gordon to no avail. On Friday the 21st day of February, 1862, Gordon was hanged, the only slave trader in the history of the United States to be tried, convicted and hanged in accordance with the Constitution and Federal law.

The same treatment was accorded Confederate Captain John Y.Beall, a member of an important Virginia family, who was tried and convicted of guerrilla warfare and of being a spy. Extraordinary pressures were exerted on the President to pardon the southerner, but he did not budge one iota. Beall met his Maker in February of 1865.

By 1900, Beall was recognized as a Confederate martyr-—a status that Gordan did not achieve.

OH, IF HE'D JUST RUN AWAY!

Many of the Unionists wanted to severely punish the Confederates, especially their leaders. They sang "Hang Jeff Davis On A Sour Apple Tree," to the tune of "John Brown's Body," and they meant it. Publicly, Abe said very little about the matter except in subtle, general terms. Privately, he was opposed to the punishing of any of our wayward brothers and was not about to make any martyrs for the Glorious Cause. His trusted cabinet members and generals knew how he felt, but they were always informed obliquely or in circumspect ways, usually by anecdote or a joke like the boy and the raccoon story:

"When I was a boy down in Indiana, one morning I walked past a cabin. A boy about my age was playing with a small coon tied to a string..'Whar'd yo get the coon,' I asked?

'Pa went a hunt'n last night and he cotched six of 'em. He done kilt five and has gone off to the mill to get some corn meal. He told me to hold on to this lit'le feller, and, when he comes home, he's surely gonna kill this little critter too. And I wish he wouldn't do it.'

"Well, if ya feel that way,why don't ya turn him loose?"

'Oh, I dasn't do that 'cause Pa would give me hell, but, oh, how I wish'd he'd just run away.'

"Now, if Jeff Davis' crowd were to just run away, or, if caught, somehow were to escape, I certainly wouldn't mind and wouldn't want to know about it."

THEY VOTED AS THEY SHOT

It looked like Lincoln would lose his bid for re-election in 1864. Between the Peace Democrats, Copperheads, conservative Republicans and those opposed to the draft and the emancipation of the blacks, his chances were slim. For four years the nation had fought the bloodiest war in all history and was weary and filled with grief.

Strangely enough, the group that had suffered the most death and deprivation, the soldiers, were for Abe. Some states allowed absentee voting for the first time, and in those that did not, those soldiers received furloughs to go home and vote. Overwhelmingly, the Union soldier went for Abe. They voted as they shot.

TURKEY FOR THE BOYS IN BLUE

During Lincoln's tenure of office, there were nine calls for prayer and thanksgiving. On July 15, 1863, ironically the third day of the brutal New York City draft riots, Abe issued a "Proclamation of Thanksgiving" to be held on Thursday the 6th day of August, for all peoples of the United States. In 1864, he re-issued the proclamation proclaiming the last Thursday of November for such a holiday, which established our traditional Thanksgiving Day.

Out of respect for that Union holiday, the Rebel troops at Petersburg, Virginia withheld their rifle fire so that Grant's men could enjoy the turkey with all of the trimmings while the rebs ate their skimpy rations.

MY POLICY IS TO HAVE NO POLICY

Abe never let policy stand in the way of getting things done. Although it drove cabinet members, Congressmen, bureaucrats and generals wild, he refused to be penned down by such dictates.

One day John Palmer, a Union Democrat from Illinois and long-time acquaintance, was allowed to see Lincoln while he was being shaved by his barber. After exchanging certain amenities, Palmer, speaking in a frank and jovial mood said, "Mr Lincoln, if anybody had told me that in a great crisis like this the people were going out to a little one-horse town and pick a one-horse town lawyer for President I wouldn't have believed it."

Whirling around with lather on his face. Lincoln put his hands on Palmer's knee and said, "Neither would I. But it was a time when a man with a policy would have been fatal to the country. I have never had a policy. I have simply tried to do what seemed best as each day came."

ABE LOVED THE GOOD BOOK

As the war progressed, Negroes came to believe that Lincoln had a personal interest in their condition and quickly grew to love and admire him. He was approachable, something that had never happened to blacks before. The "latch string" now hung out at the White House. Black leaders were welcome. He listened to their concerns and granted their requests if possible.

As an expression of their gratitude for Old Abe, the loyal black people of Baltimore took up a collection and purchased an expensive Bible as a present for him. The gift was presented by black clergymen on the lawn of the White House on July 4, 1864.* Upon receiving their ornate *Bible* he said, "In regard to this Great Book, I have but to say, it is the best gift God has given to man. All the good the Saviour gave to the world was communicated through this book. But for it we could not know right from wrong. All things most desirable for man's welfare, here and hereafter, are to be found portrayed in it."

As far as Abe was concerned, his comment expressed his feelings about the Good Book. Even a cursory study of Lincoln's speaking and writing style reveals the numerous ways in which the *Bible* influenced him. He constantly quoted scripture, and his Second Inaugual is recognized by those who have studied it as a theological classic.

*This *Bible* is in The Fisk University Library at Nashville, Tennessee. Originally, Fisk was an all black college. It was given to the college by Robert Todd Lincoln in 1916.

A LITTLE GUN THAT CAN NOT HURT

The people of this country never tire of the numerous expressions of Abe Lincoln's love for his children. Tad is the object of most of these incidents, because the Lincoln's beloved third son, Willie, died in February, 1862. The fourth son had ready access to his Father, and Abe couldn't deny Tad's requests. Most of those requests required a written order from the President ordering a government employee to satisfy the child's desires.

When Tad wanted a canon from the navy, Abe wrote the following note:

"Capt. Dahlgren may let 'Tad' have a little gun that he cannot hurt himself with."

Today the note and the small brass canon it procured are the subjects of the sweet display in the Illinois State Historical Library at Springfield.

ACCENT THE POSITIVE

As the end of the Civil War approached, special consideration was given to the oath that southern rebels must take to resume their citizenship within the Union. A big battle developed between the radical Republican Congressmen and President Lincoln. That element wanted oaths which were negatively worded demanding that the man swear that he had not been a rebel and would never be one again, etc.

Abe disliked such an oath, and on February 5th, 1864, he sent the following note to Secretary of War, Stanton; it is a classic example of Lincoln's practical wisdom tinctured by compassion: "On principle I dislike an oath which requires a man to swear he has not done wrong. It rejects the Christian principle of forgiveness on terms of repentance. I think it is enough if the man does no wrong hereafter."

ABE LOVES MARY

Before Abe met Mary Todd Lincoln he had been briefly engaged to a young woman in New Salem, Illinois by the name of Mary Owens. Sensing that he was not ready for marriage, she broke off the engagement. Thereafter, according to legend, Abe found the name of Mary a little depressing whenever he heard it spoken and on an early date asked Miss Todd if he could call her Molly.

The Lincolns' courtship was rather lengthy and turbulent. By mutual consent they called off their first wedding date set for January 1, 1841. This was probably due to the Todd's opposition to the union and Abe's pain at not being accepted by Mary's family. Without her family's approval, almost two years later, they got married.

A few weeks before Lincoln died he expressed his love for his wife. "We've been married for nearly twenty three years, and my Molly's as handsome now as when she was a girl, and I a poor nobody then fell in love with her, and, what is more, I've never fallen out." Madam, when is the last time your husband of twenty three years described you in such sweet terms?

ABE'S NEW DEAL DINER

The Republican Party that rode into Washington with Abe Lincoln in 1861 was a rare blend of self interest and altruism. Long frustrated by Southerners and certain elements of the Democratic Party, they applied federal power to aid the prince and the pauper.

Their legacy was a cornucopia of rights and institutions, many of which remain today. The Homestead Act, long derisively assailed by southerners as a sop to northern paupers, was passed, providing free farms. The Agricultural and Machinery Colleges were created allowing educational opportunity to talented, poor youth, and Gallaudet University was charted to help the blind and the deaf. Our greatest industry, agriculture, was encouraged by the creation of its own

department. Business and industry were furthered with transcontinental railroads, oceanic cables, tariffs and National Banks. And the capstone to this largess was the freeing of the slaves and saving the union.

Three constitutional amendments were added by those liberal Republicans, hopefully designed to prevent the states from destroying what they wrought. Never again would a state enslave a man or deny him the vote because of his race. All citizens were entitled to due process and the equal protection of the law. They endeavored to turn Scripture upside down by refusing to accept that "the poor will be with you always" and "(to give) to him who haveth not (rather than) to taketh away."

GOD LOVES THE POOR BECAUSE HE MADE SO MANY OF THEM

Frequently, popular quotations credited to Lincoln cannot be substantiated by concrete fact. According to John Hay, one of Lincoln's secretaries, "God loves the poor, because He created so many of them," came from one of Old Abe's dreams. Hay is the only source of its origin, and it is a maybe.

Regardless of its source, the public has appreciated this quote said in jest but filled with humorous irony. The incidents in his life and much of the major legislation of his administration were devoted to helping the poor and the reversal of this sad fact. His behavior toward the "have-nots" was certainly in harmony with the teachings of Christianity and other major religions.

ABE AUDITONS FOR THE GREAT POET'S SOCIETY

Abe loved poetry and spent many hours studying his favorite poets. From the days of his youth until his passing he strove to become a poet. His poems are poor to mediocre and usually filled with melancholy, longing and sadness.

In his youth he wrote bits of doggrel about himself and the status of women, comic burlesques about the Grigsby Brothers and incidents and events that happened in the Pigeon Creek Indiana area. While there, Abe penned a sad poem about schoolmate Matthew Gentry's sudden, violent attack of devastating mental illness. He considered him a victim of misfortune. Years later, Lincoln revisited southwest Indiana and wrote another lengthy poem about the region, again mentioning poor Matthew, now withdrawn in quiet madness. As the following lines indicate, Abe had second thoughts about the teenager's fate:

But here's an object more of dread
Than ought the grave contains
Of human form with reason fled.
While wretched life remains..."

Abe was a bit more successful as an amateur poet than as a singer, but remember, he couldn't sing for sour apples. Never accepted into the great poets' society, Lincoln has occasionally been allowed to associate with some of his beloved poets. On the campus of New York University is the Hall of Fame of Great Americans. Assembled within that memorial are busts of Lincoln and the following pride of American poetic lions: Longfellow, Lowell, Whittier, Bryant, Holmes and Whitman. In that revered sanctuary Abe's favorite poets are quite compatible keeping company with their admired politician.

ON PROMISES

Abe Lincoln, like all good politicians, believed in honoring his promises and kept them. However, being the practical person that he was, his feet were never set in concrete, and if conditions changed or new facts were revealed, occasionally he broke a promise. His actions were always motivated by what he considered to be the best solution for that moment.

This philosophical aspect of Lincoln was artfully stated in his last public address when he said,"... as bad promises are better broken than kept, I shall treat this as a bad promise, and break it whenever I shall be convinced that keeping it is adverse to the public interest."

GOD KNOWS WHICH WAS RIGHT

War is always a dirty business, and civil war is dirtier. The limited restraints of the conventional warfare between nations are often missing. The surge of passions—hate, fear, anguish and the urge to retaliate—are more intense for all who are involved, even the leaders. Lincoln rose above these passions as revealed in his Gettysburg and Second Inaugural Addresses and the numerous calls to national prayer and thanksgiving. In them he appealed to all of the people and never excluded the enemy.

Even such an ardent foe of the Union as General John B. Gorden had his moments of doubt regarding the justification of the war. In later life, he could never forget the Kentucky father who lost both of his sons in the war. One died fighting for the Union and the other for the South. The distraught father lovingly erected a joint monument over the graves of his two sons inscribed, "God knows which was right."

IT KEEPS ON PLAYING AND PLAYING AND PLAYING

They hanged Old John Brown for his Harpers Ferry Raid, but his soul kept right on marching. A martyr to those who disliked slavery and a friend of some very important and wealthy abolitionists, parodies to his memory were soon being sung to the tune of the old Methodist hymn, "On Canaan's Happy Shore."

Julia Ward Howe, wife of one of the most powerful abolitionists in the country and a backer of John Brown, was in Washington with abolitionist friends to visit with Lincoln. While there they sang fragments of popular army songs like "John Brown's Body Lies A Moldering in the Grave."

A friend encouraged her to write some better words. That night she quickly wrote all five verses of the poem and sold it to the *Atlantic Monthly* for five dollarsv.The poem was popularized by Union Army Chaplain Charles Caldwell McCabe. He had taught the poem to fellow prisons of war in Libby Prison at Richmond, Virginia. After he was released, he sang the song many times to raise money for the chaplain's fund. At a performance following Gettysburg, President Lincoln was in the audience. When McCabe finished, Abe stood up with tears in his eyes and asked him to sing it again. For most of us the trilogy of the Battle Hymn of the Republic, our reflections about the Civil War and Abe Lincoln are intertwined and inseparable. As we sing "His soul keeps marching on," we are usually smitten with a surge of warm sentiment about our country and the man who saved it, Abe Lincoln.

PARDONING ALL DESERTERS

Consistent with Abe's desire for a humane and speedy return to peace for all Americans as stated in his Second Inaugural Address, he issued a proclamation on March 11, 1865, pardoning all army deserters if they would return to their old units, no matter what had been the reason for their flight.

AARON COPLAND'S LINCOLN PORTRAIT

" Fellow
citizens, we can-
not escape history.
We of this Congress and this administration will be remembered in spite of ourselves. No personal significance of insignificance
can spare one or another of us. The fiery trial through
which we pass will light down in honor or dishonor to the
latest generation. We - even we here- hold the power and
bear the responsibility."- *State of the Union Address, Dec.
1, 1862.* "The dogmas of the quiet past are inadequate to the
stormy present. The occasion is piled high with difficulty, and
we must rise to the occasion. As our case is new, so we must
think anew and act anew. We must disenthrall ourselves and
then we shall save our country." - *State of the Union Address.
Dec. 1, 1862.* "It is the eternal struggle between two principles --
right and wrong-- throughtout the world. It is the same spirit that
says: 'You toil and work and earn bread - and I'll eat it -no matter
what shape it comes, whether from the mouth of a king who
seeks to bestride the people of his own nation and live by
the fruit of their labor, or from one race of men as an apo-
logy for enslaving another race, it is the same tyrannical
principle." - *Last Lincoln-Douglas Debate, October 15,
1858.* "As I would not be a slave, so I would not be
master, whatever differs from this, to the extent of the
difference is no de-MOC-racy." - *Fragment, c 1854.*
"..that from these honored dead we take increased
devotion to that cause for which they gave
their last full measure of devo tion;
that we here highly resolve that
these dead shall not have died in
vain; and that this nation under God,
shall have a new birth of freedom; and that
government of the people, by the
people, and for the people shall
not perish from the earth."
*Gettysburg Address,
November 19, 1863.*

A BLENDING OF ART AND POLITICS

A REGULAR SORT OF GUY

Although Abe Lincoln is the subject of more books than any other person in modern history, not much is known about his physical traits, personal habits and tastes. Conventional wisdom states that he was tall, slim, a great rough and tumble fighter, occasionally suffered from hypochondria or fits of depression, had a mole on his face, wore a beard, told stories and liked fried green apples. Where the apples came from is a mystery, but they abound in children's books.

Observations by his personal secretaries, Hay and Nicolay, during his White House Days shed some light on the subject. Lincoln suffered from insomnia. Usually, he went to bed at midnight or later, and, after a "sleep light and capricious," he arose at first light and by seven was at work in his office.

Apparently, he was not a food person. In other words he ate to live rather than lived to eat. Breakfast at nine was an egg and cup of coffee; lunch in the early afternoon, a glass of milk and a biscuit; and for dinner, he ate lightly from one or two courses. Such a diet was not the most healthful and contributed to chronic constipation. For years he took blue mass pills—a powerful chemical laxative made from mercury. So Abe was an irregular, regular fellow, and with his credibility, the hucksters from Madison Avenue and their clients would love him.

ABE'S WEB FOOTED SQUADRON

At the onset of the Civil War the South didn't have a navy, and the Union's was rather obsolete and didn't fulfill its needs. In time the South would build a small navy constructed with innovative ideas that modernized naval warfare, and the North responded with a powerful force that strangled rebel trade on the high seas and helped opened the Mississippi Valley to Union control.

Both navies had good leadership who understood what it would take to win the war much better than did their army counterparts. Confederate Secretary of the Navy, Stephen Mallory, was an early convert to iron clads and a most effective administrator, as were Gideon Wells and Under Secretary Gustavus Fox for the Union. As a result of their experimentation with iron clads and steam powered ships, all of the navies of the world were obsolete by the conclusion of the Civil War. The South had the ideas but inadequate resources. The Union with its wealth was able to respond most effectively to those new ideas and made an immense contribution toward winning the war.

Lincoln encouraged the growth of the Union Navy and appreciated its contribution to the war effort. As usual, he described its accomplishments in his colorful way. In a letter to Congressman James Conkling, August 26, 1863, he wrote: "...Nor must Uncle Sam's web feet be forgotten. At all the watery margins they have been present. Not only on the deep sea, the broad bay, and the rapid river, but also up the narrow muddy bayou, and wherever the ground was a little damp, they have been, and made their tracks..."

ABE'S LITTLE GIRL SCULPTOR

During the last five months of Lincoln's life he posed before 17 year old Vinnie Ream for a bust. Initially, he had refused to sit for her and then relented when he learned that she was a poor girl struggling on her own. Abe's last sitting was on Good Friday afternoon, April 14, 1865, the day of his assassination. He died before the clay sculpture was completed. Ream recalled later that she was "...still under the spell of his kind eyes and genial presence..." at the time that he was assassinated. She remembered Lincoln as a "...man of unfathomable sorrow."

At the age of eighteen, Vinnie was commissioned by the United States Congress to make the true-to-life statue of Abraham Lincoln which stands in the rotunda of the U. S. Capitol. She was the first woman and youngest artist to ever receive such a commission. So she was Abe's little girl sculptor.

MORE THAN HALF RIGHT

As Ward Lamon said, Abe used his stories as a laugh cure for a drooping friend, for his own melancholy or to clinch an argument and lay bare a fallacy, to disarm an antagonist. But most often the stories were "labor saving contrivances." He was not the first man in history to realize the value of a story—a parable—to get across a very apparent truth. He could always see the humor in a situation and reacted accordingly. Most of the time the persons involved enjoyed his responses.

One day Abe was in the receiving line at the White House and was shaking hands with guests when the following exchange took place:

Guest: "Mr. President. I am glad to take the hand of the man, who, with the help of Almighty God will put down this rebellion.

Abe: "You are more than half right, Sir."

IT WON'T TAKE LONG

Upon seeing an old acquaintance, Abe customarily asked, "Tell what you know. It won't take long." The usual response was a back slap, a hand shake and hearty guffaw. It was hickish and countrified but filled with amicable warmth and genuine affection. No one was offended, It was just another old country ruse that friends and neighbors pulled on one another.

However, some others found the salutation offensive, especially pompous members of Congress and officials of the government, erudite, well-to-do easterners and those individuals enamoured with their self worth. When Lincoln sprang it on liberal Republican Senator of Ohio Ben Wade or Secretary of the Treasury Salmon Chase, they grimaced and were inwardly infuriated. Was this greeting an automatic response from years of practice and said in jest? Was Abe deliberately badgering powerful individuals whose support he needed to successfully enact his programs but whom he knew were constantly plotting to bring about his downfall? Probably both, but knowing that Abe was a man who always thought before he spoke or acted, most likely the latter.

ABE'S LAST TRICK: CHINA'S OPEN DOOR

John Hay learned his politics from one of the greatest politicians of all time, Abe Lincoln. As Secretary of State for the McKinley Administration, he pulled one of the cleverest coups on the world's most powerful nations regarding the independence of China and United States access to its trade.

By 1900, it appeared that China would be divided into colonial territories of the major European powers and Japan. Fearing that possibility and realizing it was not in the best interest of the United States, Hay intervened. Privately he wrote those competing powers to guarantee China's continued existence and allow all nations to its trade. None were will-ing to publicly acknowledge the dismemberment of China and played it coy. Assuming that at least one country would say no to Hay's suggestions, they all replied that if every other nation would agree, so would the respondent. Taking their responses as a yes, Hay proclaimed the Open Door Policy for China.

Having trapped themselves, the chagrined major powers reluctantly abided by Hay's declaration. It was a smashing diplomatic success for the US, launching a fifty year period of friendship with China. The technique was pure Lincoln. Was the Open Door Policy Abe's last trick?

Charlie B

SHOES FOR TAD'S HORSE

One day a blacksmith was shoeing horses for the cavalry unit that resided on the White House grounds and served as an escort and guard for the President. Tad was watching J. F. Allen, the farrier, going about his business and asked him to shoe his horse. Very busy and not wanting to be bothered by the youth, Allen told Tad that he was doing government work and could not shoe his horse without an order from the President. Little did he realize the influence of the boy.

Tad went to his father's office and quickly returned with the note ordering the blacksmith to shoe his horse. There is no record as to how Allen shoed the horse, but the farrier kept the note:

April, 7, 1864

Shoe Tad's horse for him.

A Lincoln

LIKE PEAS IN A POD

Before Virginia seceded from the union, Abe Lincoln had offered Robert E. Lee a commanding position with the United States Army. When Virginia left, Lee remained loyal to his native state, and the Union paid a very dear price for the loss of this outstanding general. Except for the temporary setback at Antietam, Lee and his Army of Northern Virginia appeared to be invincible. His string of victories began in early '62 with the Seven Days' battles and continuing with Second Bull Run, Fredericksburg, Chancellorsville and ending with a stalemate at Gettysburg. He had outwitted and outfought them all: McClellan, Pope, Burnside, Hooker and Meade, to a degree. They were different men, but all of one mind. Abe had appointed them in his desperate search to find a winning general, and all of them had failed.

PRACTICAL ARTS COLLEGES

During most of Abe's life, he felt inadequate because of his "spotty" education. In particular he resented the arrogant attitude frequently displayed by those who had received a college education at a prestigious college. Many prominent judges, lawyers, congressmen and even members of his cabinet considered themselves his superior and made fun of his backwoods demeanor and crude pronunciation. Lincoln was a country hick and bush leaguer who went over well on the frontier but had no business in polite society. They mistook style for substance. Stanton, his Secretary of War, had been very rude to him during the McCormack Case.

For Lincoln, a college education had a practical purpose and was not an endeavor that generated snob appeal. He gladly signed the Morrill Act which gave every state the opportunity to establish a practical arts college. Large land grants were given by the federal government to help found what are known as Agricultural and Machinery Colleges. These A&M schools have provided low cost, quality educations to talented children of working people, farmers and small town businessmen for nearly a century and a half. Their product has been engineers, farmers, teachers, doctors, etc., and has fulfilled one of the dreams of the Republicans that Old Abe took with him to Washington, DC in 1861. An interesting result of this federal encouragement to establish colleges was that many states provided practically free college educations for young adults before providing for free tax supported high schools for teenagers.

I'D LOSE ANOTHER LEG FOR A MAN LIKE THAT!

A reception was held on the evening of March 4, 1865, following the Inauguration. For three hours Lincoln continuously shook hands with over 6,000 persons. Miss Adelaide Smith, a nurse, and her very close friend, Lt. Gosper, were among those received. Gosper was on crutches, having lost a leg in a skirmish before Petersburg. Adelaide had been his nurse. Swept along by the crowd, Smith and Gosper finally saw the President. To their surprise Abe stepped out before the two of them, took Gosper by the hand and in an unforgettable voice said, "God bless you, my boy!"

As the two of them moved on, the young man, ecstatic and in tears, said to his lover, "Oh! I'd lose another leg for a man like that!"

OLD ABE WASN'T THAT OLD AFTER ALL

After his inauguration in March of '65, Lincoln was physically exhausted and took to bed for a few days. Although only 56 years of age, to many people he appeared old and worn down. Josh Speed, his oldest and dearest friend, was at the inauguration. He had not seen him for a long time and was worried about Abe's run down condition. Mary, his friends and secretaries encouraged him to do less official work and to go to the theater, take carriage rides and to rest, which he did.

In late March he left the capitol and commenced a fortnight visit with the army around Petersburg and Richmond. Before returning to Washington, he regained his strength and was in good spirits.

One of the last things he did before returning to Washington was to chop some wood and then put on a little show for the men. To their delight, he took the ax by the end of the handle with his right hand and held it straight out and horizontal to the ground without a shake or quiver—a great display of stength. After he left, some strong soldiers attempted to duplicate the same feat and failed. The people lovingly talked and sang about Old Abe Lincoln, but that April day, less than a week before his death, he wasn't that old!

WE MUST HANG ON TO THE REBELS

On the night of April 11th, as President Lincoln stood in a candle lighted window above the White House portico and delivered his last speech, someone in the crowd asked, "What shall we do with the Rebels?" A raucous voice answered, "Hang them!" Abe's youngest son, Tad, who was standing near his father, quickly replied, "Oh, no, we must hang on to them." "That's right," said Lincoln, "we must hang on to them."

The spontaneous, profound response of this impish twelve year old gave his father another opportunity to reaffirm Lincoln's consistent position of a humane and compassionate treatment for the vanquished Southern brothers.

THINGS ARE LOOKING UP, MOLLY

Abe's and Molly's relationship had greatly improved during their last few weeks together. With Lee's surrender and the adjournment of the Congress until December '65, much of the stress and political pressure on Lincoln was off. Mary felt that her husband would have more time to share with her. They had an intimate breakfast that fatal April 14th morning with their son, Robert. Their oldest son was engaged to Mary Harlan, daughter of Abe's new Secretary of the Interior. Maybe the Lincolns would soon be grandparents.

Just before dinner the two of them had a buggy ride and were making plans for the future again. After finishing his second term they wanted to travel, possibly to England and the Holy Land, before returning to Springfield. Abe looked forward to practicing law and settling down on a prairie farm on the banks of the Sangamon River where he planned to live out the rest of his days as an elder statesman for his country. Following dinner they were going to the theater.

Things were certainly looking up on that Good Friday for the Lincolns and the nation.

LAST MEETING IN THE UPPER OFFICE

Lincoln arose Good Friday Morning 1865, in great spirits, having enjoyed a rare night of sound sleep. As he opened the windows of the second story room which he called his shop, Abe could see that the Dogwood and Judas trees were in bloom and detected the scent of spring flowers. At eight he had an intimate breakfast with Molly and Robert. He felt good and had a lot to feel great about. He had been overwhelmingly re-elected president, the Republican Party had picked up seats in the Congress, the Thirteenth Amendment abolishing slavery was now being ratified by the states and his cabinet was composed of men of his own choosing. Finally, for the first time since he was inaugurated, Abe did not have to worry about secession and rebellion. He looked forward to the cabinet meeting with a sense of anticipation and accomplishment.

General Grant and his son, Robert, attended the meeting where plans were discussed about the reconstruction. "I think it is providential," he remarked, "that this great rebellion is crushed just as Congress has adjourned and there are none of the disturbing elements of that body to hinder and embarrass us." Now they could concentrate on the future and the implementation of the programs promised in 1860. Yes, it appeared to be a great day...

Oates, 462-466; War Years, 829-833.

LAURA KEENE'S LAST ROLE FOR ABE

Following the brief incapacitating shock of realizing that the President had been shot, youthful Dr. Charles Leale, an expert on gunshot wounds, arrived at Lincoln's box and proceded to examine him. He quickly concluded that the President had received a mortal wound. Leale used his finger to remove the clot blocking drainage from the gunshot wound and with the assistance of Dr. Charles Taft administered mouth to mouth resuscitation which revived the comatose Lincoln's labored breathing.

Others soon arrived at the President's box. Among them was the play's leading lady,

Laura Keene, who brought a pitcher of water and emotionally begged to hold the dying man's head in her lap and bathe his face. The actress sat on the floor oblivious to the blood that stained her beautiful satin dress and tenderly and uselessly sprinkled his ashen face until the decision was made to move the mortally wounded Lincoln. Thus Miss Keene performed the last and saddest role of her career for the man who loved the theater and Shakespeare.

THE OTHER PRESIDENT AT FORD'S THEATER

GOOD FRIDAY. 1865

Strange as it may seem, there was another president at Ford's Theater on the evening of April 14th, 1865. About eleven thirty that Good Friday morning, a presidential messenger arrived at the theater informing its management that the President had accepted their invitation to attend the evening's performance of Our American Cousin.

Desiring to make the President comfortable, the Ford Brothers immediately set about redecorating and furnishing an enlarged box for his party. Two regular boxes were combined and special furniture was moved in, including a large rocking chair for Abe. Flags draped its sides with the bunting suspended beneath the windows. In the middle of the bunting and affixed to the upright which divided the regular boxes was a large, framed engraving of George Washington. Yes, the Father of Our Country was there to view in sad disbelief the end of its savior.

MOLLY'S CHILD'S PART

"The shoe maker's kids do without shoes," goes the old adage. Iron-ically, this bit of wisdom rings true. The cobbler's family, like those of many other professions, is the last to get service. As good a lawyer as Lincoln was, he left Mary without a will. Why? Who knows? No doubt he certainly had more reasons not to have drafted one than most of us, but he failed to follow the most trenchant bit of advice given by the members of the bar—be sure and make out a will!

Lincoln's estate was tied up for three years before being settled. His long-time personal, legal and political friend, Supreme Court Justice David Davis, handled the estate. When it was finally settled, Mary got the customary, common-law child's part.

BLACK EASTER '65

The unexpected assassination of Lincoln left the nation in shock, catapulting its people into twenty days of mental anguish and bereavement. Everywhere, people clustered together to find support and comfort and share a grief intensified by remembrances of a heart so tender and merciful struck down in the hour of triumph.

The Easter holiday had dawned bright that Good Friday of '65, with victory and anticipations of a glorious peace skillfully directed by Old Abe. It ended with a vast gloom and sadness indelibly imprinted in that generation's memory as Black Easter. Something happened to the national psyche, and a new world hero was elevated to perpetual immortality among the pantheon of gods.

In a letter Abe stated his conviction regarding what he considered to be the proper earthly behavior of a Christian intent on getting into heaven.

"When brought to my final reckoning," he wrote, "may I have to answer for robbing no man of his goods; yet more tolerable even this, than for robbing one of HIMSELF, and ALL that was HIS."

MOVE OVER GEORGE!

Even before his death, Lincoln was constantly coupled and compared with Washington. Early in our history George Washington, as Father of His Country, had been elevated to godly status by his countrymen and much of the world. With Abe's assassination, a Savior of the Nation was born, and George had company. Both are in that rare pantheon of earthly beings cherished by mankind throughout the world.

While we are a very religious people in this country and do not build temples to gods, we do to men: Washington, Lincoln and, to a degree, Tom Jefferson! Although these men are ours, the world also claims and honors them. Monuments to them are everywhere, Washington, DC to Liverpool and London, England; Mount Vernon to Mount Rushmore; from the Tia Juana River to the Potomac. They are expressions of love, respect and affection from a predominant majority of all of our fellow creatures.

APPENDICES

ABE'S GOT TO HAVE A BEARD

Most of the time Abe Lincoln will appear in this book with his beard, even though the event took place when he was beardless. I confess to this historical distortion, because an overwhelming majority of mankind would not recognize him sans beard, and it is my sincere desire that every person who opens this book easily recognizes Old Abe and enjoys a greater understanding of this rare man.

I made this discovery as a tender youth of eighteen in 1945, while on a noble mission to take democracy to the oppressed masses throughout much of the world. I was able to interact and exchange ideas and goods with many cultures and racial groups. All of these people had their heroes and religious leaders whose likenesses were sought after and cherished by the faithful. To my amazement, I discovered that universally

there were two other men whose pictures were coveted more—George Washington under wig, and Abe Lincoln with a beard. Never had I seen such expressions of genuine desire, enthusiastic commitment and unbridled avarice, especially if those likenesses appeared on rectangular pieces of paper approximately two inches wide and six inches long and colored a particular shade of green. (A green color given to the world by Abe as a result of the Civil War.) The lust to acquire them has compromised nations' integrity, sacrificed their daughters' and wives' virtue and even encouraged murder.

A half century later, I have my doubts about our success at democratizing the world, but of this I am certain: Abe has to have a beard. Other wise, the world will not give his likeness currency.

LOOK'N FOR THE LOST SPEECH

Did Abe Lincoln ever deliver an address known as his "Lost Speech"? If he did, where did he deliver it? What was lost? The original manuscript? If someone offered to sell you the original, would you buy it? Or is the whole issue a humbug?

Honestly, Abe did deliver his "Lost Speech" at the conclusion of the organizational meeting of the Illinois State Republican Party held at Bloomington, Illinois, May 29th, 1856. A new party composed of a duke's mixture of conservative and Know Nothing Whigs, anti-Nebraska Democrats, abolitionists and Germans was formed. This action delighted Lincoln. Without a script or notes he extemporaneously delivered what has been acclaimed the greatest speech of his life. Even a politician's most sceptical critics— newspaper reporters—put down their pens and, like the new partisans, were mesmerized by his oratory. Only a brief report in the Alton Currier gave the highlights of the speech. Since there were no draft, notes or coverage, no copy exists, and it became known as his "Lost Speech".

If you bought the manuscript, you have fulfilled the cynical destiny of P. T. Barnum's classic quote about separating a fool from his money. Such an offer has been made at least once, and I turned it down.

ON THE GETTYSBURG ADDRESS

The Gettysburg Address is a unique creation shrouded in its own mystique. It continues to grow, attracting facts, half truths and myths. The speech is acknowledged as one of the most eloquent speeches ever presented in English and is probably the most popular piece of prose in history. Memorized by millions since its delivery on November 19, 1863, the purpose of its original message and impact have been, for the most part, either overlooked, ignored or misconstrued. With the possible exception of "In the beginning," "Four score and" is the most frequently quoted, attention getting phrase in the United States. Almost everyone recognizes it. However, when the words are translated into other languages, it loses its unique character and becomes just plain eighty–seven.

Today few know why Lincoln was at Gettysburg. He willingly accepted the invitation to attend and deliver a few appropriate words at the dedication of the Gettysburg Military Cemetery. He wanted to restate the Civil War's aims and do a little political fence mending. Abe knew that there would be a huge crowd at the ceremonies, because eighteen Union states had participated in the cemetery's construction, loved ones would come to honor their deceased kin and Edward Everett, as principle speaker, was a great crowd pleaser. Abe's popularity was at its lowest ever due to his issuance of the Emancipation Proclamation, freeing the slaves, implementation of the draft earlier in 1863, and the continuing sacrifices of the war. Maybe the dedication would provide him with an audience willing to listen to his justification for those actions. Delivered in plain, simple English and employing a classical Greek cadence, Lincoln relied upon the equality clause of the Declaration of Independence as his guiding light for freeing men and saving the Union. Abe pulled it off, and mankind experienced an unforgettable, cherished event.

Some scholars have been interested in an analysis of the structure of the speech. Knowing Lincoln's favorite subjects were grammar and Euclidean Geometry, there are some who contend that the speech is written like a classical, geometric proof. According to them, all sentences are connected by similar words and ideas to each other. With exception of the first and last sentences, the remaining eight are connected to the preceding and following statements. A closer study of this beloved Address does tend to substantiate this contention. It would also explain his repetition of certain phrases and words. The following page has the speech broken down a sentence at a time and displays the author's application of this theory. The reader is encouraged to conduct the same experiment.

THE AUTHOR'S GEOMETRIC ANALYSIS
OF THE GETTYSBURG ADDRESS

Four score and seven years ago our fathers brought forth on this continent, _a new nation, conceived_ in Liberty and <u>dedicated</u> to the proposition that all men are created equal.

Now we are engaged in <u>A GREAT CIVIL WAR,</u> testing whether **that nation,** or any nation **_so conceived_** and **_so dedicated,_** can long endure.

We are met on a great _<u>battle field</u>_ of **THAT WAR.**

We have come to _dedicate_ a portion of **_that field,_** as a final resting place for those who here gave their lives that that nation might live. It is altogether fitting and proper that we should do this.

But, in a larger sense, we can not _dedicate_—we can not _consecrate_—-we cannot hallow—this ground.

The brave men, living and dead, _<u>who struggled here,</u>_ have **consecrated** it far above our poor power to add or detract. The world will little note, nor long remember, what we say here, but it can never forget what they did here.

It is for us, the living, rather, to be _dedicated_ here to the unfinished work which they **_who fought here_** have thus far so nobly advanced.

It is, rather, for us to be here **dedicated** to the great task remaining before us—- that from _THESE HONORED DEAD_ we take increased devotion to that cause for which they gave the last full measure of **devotion,** that we here highly resolve that **_THESE DEAD_** shall not have died in vain—-that this nation, under God, shall have a new birth of freedom—-and that government of the people, by the people, for the people, shall not perish from the earth.

1. _<u>nation</u>_ 2. **nation** 3. _nation_

Letters

Letter to Fanny Mc Cullough

Executive Mansion,
Washington, December 23, 1862.

Dear Fanny
It is with deep grief that I learn of the death of your kind and
brave father; and, especially, that it is affecting your young heart
beyond what is common in such cases. In this sad world of ours,
sorrow comes to all; and, to the young, it comes with bitterest agony, because it takes them unawares. The older have learned to
ever expect it. I am anxious to afford some alleviation of your
present distress. Perfect relief is not possible, except with time.
You cannot now realize that you will ever feel better. Is not this
so? And yet it is a mistake. You are sure to be happy again. To
know this, which is certainly true, will make you some less miserable now. I have had experience enough to know what I say; and
you need only to believe it, to feel better at once. The memory of
your dear father, instead of an agony, will yet be a sad sweet feeling in your heart, of a purer, and holier sort than you have known
before.
Please present my kind regards to your afflicted mother.

Your sincere friend,

A. Lincoln

Letter to Mrs. Bixby

Executive Mansion,

Washington, Nov. 21, 1864.

Dear Madam,
I have been shown in the files of the War Department a statement
of the Adjutant General of Massachusetts, that you are the
mother of five sons who have died gloriously on the field of battle.
I feel how weak and fruitless must be any words of mine which
should attempt to beguile you from the grief of a loss so overwhelming. But I cannot refrain from tendering to you the consolation
that may be found in the thanks of the Republic they died to save.
I pray that our Heavenly Father may assuage the anguish of
your bereavement, and leave you only the cherished memory of
the loved and lost, and the solemn pride that must be yours, to
have laid so costly a sacrifice upon the altar of freedom. Yours,
very sincerely and respectfully,

A Lincoln

VALUABLE QUOTES

Abe's writings and speeches are loaded with excellent quotations that can be the topic of a good talk, a meaningful note to a friend, used to convince an opponent in an argument or for a debate. It is hoped that this limited list will be helpful to the reader. The footnotes are for the more serious student interested in source materials.

1. History is philosophy teaching by example.

2. Shall he, who cannot do much, be, for that reason, excused if he do nothing?

3. ...the influence of fashion...(is)...but the influence that other people's actions have on our own actions...

4. If you would win a man to your cause, first convince him that you are his sincere friend.

5. After an angry and dangerous controversy, the parties made friends by dividing the bone of contention.

6. Stand with anybody that stands right. Stand with him while he is right and part with him when he goes wrong.

7. Will springs from the two elements of moral sense and self-interest.

8. The principles of Jefferson are the definitions and axioms of free society.

9. With public sentiment, nothing can fail; without it nothing can succeed.

10. The Democracy (Democrats) of today hold the liberty of one man to be absolutely nothing, when in conflict with another man's right to property. Republicans, on the contrary, are for both the man and the dollar; but in cases of conflict, the man before the dollar.

11. He (Douglas) never lets the logic of principle, displace the logic of success.

12. ...education (is) cultivated thought...

13. Every blade of grass is a study; and to produce two, where there was but one, is both a profit and a pleasure.

14. On book learning: A capacity, and taste, for reading, gives access to whatever has already been discovered by others. It is the... already solved problems .

15. Human action can be modified to some extent, but human nature cannot be changed.

16. Are all the laws, save one, to go unexecuted, and the government itself go to pieces, lest that one be violated?

17. No men living are more worthy to be trusted than those who toil up from poverty-none less inclined to take, or touch, aught which they have not honestly earned.

18. Never sell out old friends to buy old enemies.

19. In my judgement, such of us as have never fallen victims,(to alcohol) have been spared more from the absence of appetite, than from any mental or moral superiority over those who have.

20. One man has as good a right to cross a river as another has to sail up or down it.

21. The leading rule for the lawyer, as for the man of every other calling, is diligence.

22. Discourage litigation...There will still be business enough.

23. As a general rule never take your whole fee in advance, nor any more than a small retainer.

VALUABLE QUOTES

24. if...you cannot be an honest lawyer, resolve to be honest without being a lawyer.

25. Understanding the spirit of our institutions to aim at the elevation of men, I am opposed to what ever tends to degrade them.

26. I meant all I said, and did not mean what I did not say.

27. I have never had a feeling, politically, that did not spring from the sentiments embodied in the Declaration of Independence.

28. I have endured a great deal of ridicule without much malice; and have received a great deal of kindness, not quite free from ridicule.

29. The Republican Party should not become "a mere sucked egg, all shell and no meat, the principle all sucked out".

30. On Government:

   A. The legitimate object of government, is to do for a community of people, whatever they need to have done, but cannot do, at all, or cannot, so well do, for themselves in their separate, and individual capacities.

   B. In all that the people can individually do as well for themselves, government ought not to interfere.

   C. ...it appears that if all men were just, there still would be some, though not so much, need of government.

31. I believe I shall never be old enough to speak without embarrassment when I have nothing to say.

32. Why should we censure a man who has done so much for his country because he did not do a little more? (Meade following Gettysburg)

33. Two men may honestly differ about a question and both be right.

34. We must look not merely to buying cheap, not yet to buying cheap and selling dear: but also to having constant employment.

35. As a general rule, I think, we would (do) much better (to) let it (the Constitution) alone. No slight occasion should tempt us to touch it (with an amendment).

36. I go for all sharing the privileges of the government, who assist in bearing its burthens. Consequently I go for admitting all whites to the right of suffrage, who pay taxes or bear arms, (by no means excluding females).

37. There is no grievance that is a fit object of redress by mob law.

38. ...let every man remember that to violate the law is to trample on the blood of his father, and to tear the charter of his own, and his children's liberty.

39. No man is good enough to govern another without the other man's consent.

40. If the minority will not acquiesce, the majority must, or the government must cease.

41. Men readily perceive that they cannot be much oppressed by a debt which they owe to themselves.

42. The most reliable indication of public purpose in this country is derived through our popular elections.

43. A jury too frequently has at least one member more ready to hang the panel than to hang the traitor.

44. Let us have faith that right makes might, and in that faith, let us to the end, dare to do our duty , as we understand it.

VALUABLE QUOTES

45. There is a difference between being paid to eat and paying for it.

46. The most valuable special ability for a winning politician is to be able to raise a cause which will produce an effect and then fight the effect.

47. I can't pull my son down by the bootstraps I pulled myself up with.

48. In giving freedom to the slave, we assure freedom for the free.

49. I...wish to be no less than National in all the positions I may take....

50. Some of you will be successful, and such will need but little philosophy....

51. The man who is of neither party, is not—cannot be of any consequence.

52. Half finished work generally proves to be labor lost.

53. Judge Lynch sometimes take(s) jurisdiction of cases which prove too strong for the courts.

54. By all means, don't say "if I can"; say "I will".

FOOTNOTES

1. Living Lincoln,150; Address before Whig Convention, 08/26/52,
2. Ibid, 53; Washington Society Lecture, 02/22/42;
3. Ibid, 53.
4. Ibid, 50.
5. Ibid, 167; Peoria Speech, 10/16/54.
6. Ibid , 176.
7. Ibid, 206; Lincoln's response to Douglas's speech supporting the Dred Scott Decision of the US Supreme Court, 06/26/57.
8. Ibid, 289; Letter to Boston Republicans 04/05/59.
9. Living Lincoln, 249; Ist Lincoln Douglas debate at Ottawa, IL. 8/21/58.
10. Ibid, 289;
11. Ibid, 296; Note c Sept. 1859.
12. Ibid, 302; Wisconsin State Fair Speech, 09/30/59.
13. Ibid, 301.
14. Ibid, 302.
15. Ibid, 315; Cooper Union Speech. 2/27/60.
16. Ibid, 417; Message to Special Session of Congress, 07/04/61.
17. Ibid, 453; State of the Union Address, 12/03/61.
18. Oates, 163.
19. Living Lincoln, 54.
20. Oates,149, Hurd v the Rock Island Bridge Company, 09/08/57.
21. Lang, 29-32; Notes For A Law Lecture, c 1850.
22. Ibid.
23. Ibid.
24. Ibid.
25. Ibid, 69; Letter to Dr. Theodore Canisius, 05/17/59.
26. Ibid, 76; Letter to O .P. Hall, J. R. Fullenwider & U. F. Correll, 02/14/60.
27. Ibid, 98; Address at Philadelphia, 02/22/61
28. Ibid, 201, Letter to James H. Hackett, Shakespearean actor.
29. War Years, 347.
30. Living Lincoln, 155.
31. War Years, 708.
32. Ibid, 362.
33. Ibid, 766.
34. Collected Works, v. 1, 411.
35. Ibid, v. 1, 488.
36. Living Lincoln, 11.
37. Ibid, 23.
38. Ibid, 23.
39. Peterson, 44.
40. Collected Works, v. 4, 268.
41. Living Lincoln, 629; State of the Union Address, 12/05/64.
42. Ibid, 630.
43. Collected Works, v. 6, 264.
44. Living Lincoln, 319, Cooper Union Address.
45. Notes.
46. Notes
47. Oates, 188.
48. Collected Works, v. 5, 537.
49. Ibid, v. 2, 248.
50. Ibid, v. 3, 481.
51. Ibid, v. 2, 126.
52. Ibid, v. 1, 5.
53. Ibid, v. 6, 396.
54. Ibid, v. 3, 90.

GLOSSARY

Abolitionist. Persons who opposed slavery in the United States.

Adversary. An opponent; the system of justice practiced in the United States by attornies opposing one another to arrive at a truthful solution.

Anecdote. A short account of an interesting or humorous incident.

Bad split. In bowling the toughest split conversion possible for a bowler -the 7 and 10 pins; rarely is it made.

Bawdy. Humorously coarse, crude, vulgar.

Blab school. Type of school Lincoln attended; students talked aloud memorizing lessons.

Black Friday. Good Friday, 4/14/65, the date Abraham Lincoln was shot.

Blue Mass pills. A pill of finely divided mercury used as a laxative.

Bung . A stopper for the hole in a cask or barrel; a drain plug.

Bunghole. The hole in a barrel through which liquid is poured in or drained out.

Bunion. A painful, inflamed swelling or growth of the first joint of the big toe.

Capital. Material wealth used in the production of more wealth.

Cerebral. Appealing to or requiring the use of the intellect; intellectual rather than emotional.

Chagrin. A keen feeling of mental unease or embarrassment.

Chickpeas. An annual Asian plant in the pea family; garbanzo beans.

Confederacy. Organization of southern states that fought the Union during the Civil War.

Congressional Medal. Highest military decoration awarded persons in the United States; created during the Civil War.

Conscription. Compulsory enrollment, especially for the armed forces; draft.

Contention. A striving to win in competition; rivalry.

Continental. Paper money or bonds issued by the US Continental Congress during the Revolutionary War.

Contraband. An escaped slave during the Civil War who fled to or was taken behind Union lines .

Conventional wisdom. Conforming to established practice or accepted standards; traditional.

Coups. A brilliantly executed stratagem; a masterstroke; to overthrow a government.

Court packing. Adding more judges to a court by the executive to get favorable decisions.

Deferment. Postponement of compulsory military service; avoiding the draft.

Deja vu. French for already seen; a feeling that you have already experienced a situation.

Diametrically. Exactly opposite; contrary.

Diligence. Earnest and persistent application to an undertaking; steady effort; get the job done.

Disdain. To regard or treat with haughty contempt; despise.

Distraught. Deeply agitated, as from emotional conflict; mad; insane.

Doggerel. Crudely or irregularly fashioned verse, often of a humorous or burlesque nature; poor poetry.

Dr. Spock. An American physician and expert on child rearing; advocated little discipline.

Emancipation Proclamation. A proclamation made by President Lincoln in 1863 freeing slaves.

GLOSSARY

Embryo. A rudimentary or beginning stage; the beginning.

Euchre. To deceive by sly or underhand means; cheat; based on term from an old card game.

Extemporaneous. Skilled at or given to unrehearsed speech.

Extremism. One who advocates or resorts to measures beyond the norm, especially in politics.

Faculty. Any of the powers or capacities possessed by the human mind .

Farrier. A blacksmith who makes shoes for horses and applies them to the hooves.

Flotation. The act, process, or condition of floating.

Gerrymander. To divide (a geographic area) into voting districts so as to give unfair advantage to one party in elections.

Great Emancipator. Name given to Lincoln for issuing the Emancipation Proclamation freeing the slaves.

Habeas corpus. A legal term requiring the police to physically present an accused person before a judge to determine if a crime has been committed; a person's greatest protection from a police state.

Horatio Alger. American late nineteenth century writer of inspirational adventure books featuring poor boys who through hard work and virtue became successful.

Horse of a different color. A different matter entirely.

Hypochondria. A persistent feeling of being ill; may actually feel pain without the illness.

Introspective. Contemplation of one's own thoughts, feelings, and sensations; self-examination.

Intuitive. Derived from or prompted by a natural tendency or impulse.

Janus. The god of gates and doorways, with two faces looking in opposite directions; two faced.

Kansas-Nebraska Act. An 1850's law allowing a proposed territory to decide whether it could come into the Union as free or slave state. Did away with the Missouri-Maine Compromise.

Litigation. To engage in legal proceedings.

Little Giant. Descriptive name given to Senator Stephan A Douglas, Lincoln's political enemy.

Loquacious. Very talkative; rambling, tiresome speech.

Malice. A desire to harm others or to see others suffer; extreme ill will or spite.

Manifest Destiny. The 19th-century doctrine that the United States had the right and duty to expand throughout the North American continent to its natural boundaries.

Mason and Dixon Line. Originally a boundary line dividing Pennsylvania and Maryland; later considered the dividing line between slave and free states within the United States until the Civil War.

Melancholy. Sadness or depression of the spirits; gloom.

Memoriam. In memory of; as a memorial.

Metes and bounds. A boundary line; a limit: metes and bounds; the legal description of a piece of land.

Missouri Compromise. Policy that determined whether states carved from the Louisiana Territory would be admitted to the Union as free or slave states; worked well until the mid 1850's.

Mystique. An aura of heightened value, interest, or meaning surrounding something; imputes a special power or mystery to an object.

No quarter. The rarely used practice of taking no prisoners in a battle; all of the defeated are killed by the victor.

Orthographical. Spelled correctly.

GLOSSARY

Pleading. A plea; an entreaty; advocacy of causes in court.

Polemics. The art or practice of argumentation or controversy; to refute errors of doctrine.

Polygraph. An instrument used as a lie detector.

Precedent. A judicial decision that may be used as a standard in similar cases.

Preclude. To exclude or prevent (someone) from a given condition or activity.

Prodigious. Impressively great in size, force, or extent; extraordinary; marvelous.

Proverbial. A short, pithy saying in frequent and widespread use that expresses a basic truth or practical precept; widely referred to, as if the subject of a proverb.

Pseudonym. A fictitious name assumed by an author; a pen name.

Rafter. One of the sloping beams that supports a pitched roof.

Redeye gravy. Gravy made from the juices of a cooked ham; very popular in the southern United States.

Ridicule. Words or actions intended to evoke contemptuous laughter at or feelings toward a person or thing.

Repository. A place where things may be put for safekeeping.

Revisionists. Persons who revise an accepted, long-standing view, especially historical events and movements.

Seceded. To withdraw formally from membership in an organization or alliance.

Shakespeare. English playwright and poet whose body of works is considered the greatest in English literature. He was Lincoln's favorite author.

Spin doctor. A representative for a person, especially a politician, who publicizes favorable interpretations of that person's words or actions.

Spot Resolutions. A series of statements attacking President Polk's reasons waging war with Mexico; presented by Congressman Abraham Lincoln.

Spotty. Lacking consistency; uneven; Lincoln's description of his education; also an uncomplimentary nickname given to Lincoln by Democrats for introducing the Spot Resolutions during the Mexican War.

Sublime. Inspiring awe; impressive; of high spiritual worth.

Sucker. Slang nickname for persons from Illinois.

Summations. A concluding part an argument containing a summary of principal points, especially of a case before a court of law.

Tabloid. A newspaper giving the news in condensed form, usually with illustrated, often sensational material.

Temperance. Restraint in the use of or abstinence from alcoholic liquors.

Tempers. To modify by the addition of a moderating element; moderate.

Tin ear. An insensitivity to music or to sounds of a given kind; can't sing or carry a tune.

Ugly duckling. One that is considered ugly at first but becomes beautiful; after the Ugly Duckling fairy tale.

Varioloid. A modified form of small pox; not as severe as original.

Vignette. A short scene or incident, as from a movie.

Whigs. One of the major political parties within the United States during the years 1828-1856.

Wigwam. Building in Chicago where Republican Convention was held in 1860.

Wilmot Proviso. A position by Lincoln's Whig party opposing the extension of slavery to any of the territory taken from Mexico as a result of the Mexican War.

BIBLIOGRAPHY

The cartoons appearing in this book are based upon the sources listed in Works Cited. Every effort has been made to ascertain the truth of the event, circumstance or quotation appearing in the cartoon and can be found in the Works Cited. Many are in print and most of them can be found in book stores or local libraries. The serious student can refer to the most recent publications quoted here and consult their bibliographies. At the bottom of almost every page is an abbreviated bibliographical entry. It is indicated in **boldface** type below. It appears there to assist the reader in locating the material on which the cartoon and commentary are based.

WORKS CITED

American Heritage*, New York: American Heritage Publishing Co., Inc., April, 1965,

Angle, Paul M., and Earl Schenck Miers. *The **Living Lincoln**.* Barnes & Noble, 1955.

Basler, Roy P., Marion Dolores Pratt, and Lloyd A. Dunlap, eds, *The **Collected Works** of*

Abraham Lincoln, 12 vols. Rutgers University Press, 1953-1990.

Boritt, Gabor S., *Of The People, By The People, For The People.* Columbia University Press, 1996.

Cornish, Dudley T. *The Sable Arm: Black Troops in the Union Army, 1861-1865.* University of Kansas, 1956.

Davis, Kenneth. *Don't Know Much About The Civil War,* William Morrow and Company, 1996.

Donald, David H. **Lincoln.** Simon & Schuster, 1995.

Donald, David H. **Liberty and Union.** D. D. Heath and Company, 1977.

Donald, David H. *Lincoln's Herndon.* Alfred Knopf, 1948.

Donovan, Frank. *Mr. Lincoln's Proclamation.* Dodd, Mead & Company, 1964.

Gladstone, William A. *Men of Color,* Thomas Publications, 1993.

Harkness, David J., and R. Gerald McMurtry. **Lincoln's Favorite Poets.** University of Tennessee Press, 1959.

Jaffa. Harry V. *Crisis Of The House Divided.* University of Chicago Press, 1959.

Kunigunde **Duncan** and D.F. Nickols Graham. *Mentor Graham: Who Taught Lincoln,* University of Chicago Press, 1945,

Lair, John. Songs Lincoln Loved. Duel, Sloan and Pearce, 1954.

Lang, H. Jack. *The Wit and Wisdom of Abraham Lincoln.* The World Publishing Company, 1941.

Lorant, Stefan. *Lincoln: A Picture History of His Life.* Harper & Brothers, 1952.

Lowry, Thomas P. *The Story the Soldiers Wouldn't Tell,* Stackpole Books, 1994.

---

*abbreviated, bibliographical page entry

May, Edith P., ed. *The Smithsonian Book of the **First Ladies**.* Henry Holt and Company, 1996.

Morison, Samuel E. and Henry Steele Commanger. *The Growth of the American Republic.* Oxford University Press, 1942.

Newhouse, Susan Nabee, *Sojourner Truth: Slave, Prophet, Legend.* New York University Press, 1995.

Oates, Stephen B. *With Malice Toward None.* Mentor Book, 1978.

Petterson, Merrill. *Lincoln In American Memory.* Oxford University Press, 1995.

Phillips, Donald T. *Lincoln On Leadership.* Warner Books, Inc., 1992.

Quarles, Benjamin. *The Negro in the Civil War.* Little, Brown and Company, 1953.

Rhodehamel, John H., and Thomas F. Schwartz. *The Last Best Hope of Earth*, Huntington Library, 1993.

Sandburg, Carl. *Abraham Lincoln, The **Prairie Years**.* Dell Publishing Co., Inc.,1968.

Sandburg, Carl. *Abraham Lincoln, The **War Years**.* Dell Publishing Co., Inc.,1968.

Trueblood, David E. *Abraham Lincoln Theologian of American Anguish.* Harper & Row, 1973.

Ward, Geoffrey C., Ric **Burns** and Ken Burns. *The Civil War, An Illustrated History.* Alfred Knopf, 1990.

Wills, Garry. *Lincoln at Gettysburg, The Words That Remade America.* Simon & Schuster, 1992.

Zall, P.M. *Abe Lincoln Laughing.* University of Tennessee Press, 1995.

WEB SITES

THE ABRAHAM LINCOLN ASSOCIATION web sit is a great place to visit. There is little need for the serious student of Lincoln to go to Springfield, Illinois, or the library when this web site is available. Its loaded and has so much. It is wise to make bookmarks from within the site. **http://www.alincolnassoc.com/**

ABRAHAM LINCOLN ONLINE is a fabulous web site. All kinds of goodies can be found. Again, it is wise to make bookmarks from within the site. **http://www.netins.net/showcase/creative/lincoln.html**

Any serious student can spend days with the above two sites . If they don't have the information you want, they have the links to lesser sites. Have fun searching the net and getting to know Abe Lincoln better.

TOPICAL INDEX OF CARTOONS

This index groups the cartoons with page numbers by topical headings for the aid and pleasure of the reader. Cartoons may be found under different topics.

TOPICAL INDEX OF CARTOONS

TOPICAL INDEX OF CARTOONS

TOPICAL INDEX OF CARTOONS

The End*

* SEE PAGE 188

ON THE AUTHOR

Charles Brame

The author, Charles Brame, bears a head-turning resemblance to Abraham Lincoln. Is this merely some happy coincidence of fate, or is there perhaps some connection of genetic material? It is possible that his ancestors co-mingled with those of Abraham Lincoln, since both are descendants of settlers from Kentucky via Virginia. Mr. Brame grew up on a farm across the Mississippi River from Lincoln's home turf. Thus, not only are the appearances of the two men similar, but they share common local language expressions, humor and philosophy from a common environment.

A long-time student of Lincoln, Brame achieved undergraduate majors in history, education and agriculture and has a Master of Arts Degree in American History from the University of Missouri. Before becoming a full time actor and writer, he taught every level from grade five through Junior College in a thirty three year teaching career in Missouri and California.

Brame has enchanted his audiences in thousands of performances as Abraham Lincoln on stage, television and movies, spreading the humour, charm and warmth of "Old Abe" while leading his viewers to a greater knowledge of Lincoln and history. A serious actor and an expert in the life and times of Lincoln, he holds memberships in Screen Actors' Guild and in the American Federation of Radio and Television Artists.

Honestly Abe won the Benjamin Franklin award for best biography in Canada and the United States in April of 1999. The book has recieved acclaim and many notable endorsements from major historians and authors.

A PERSONAL MESSAGE TO THE READER

If you enjoyed Charles Brame's *HONESTLY ABE* and wish to share it with others, order extra copies for your relatives, friends, and business associates. It will make an excellent gift for the Civil War and Lincoln buff, birthdays, thanks to a gracious host, or for that hard to please person dear to you. Upon request the author will gladly sign it, thereby enhancing its value.

REPRODUCE OR COPY THIS ORDER FORM:

FAX: (909) 989-0506

TELEPHONE ORDERS: (888) 713-9919

POSTAL ORDERS: ABE Press, P.O. Box 521-2,
Alta Loma, CA 91701-521 USA
Tel: (909) 944-5438

PRICE
 HDB: $24.95   PB: $14.95

Please send ___ copy(s) of HONESTLY ABE: **Amount**_____

Name:_____

Street _____

City:_____State:_____Zip:_____

Telephone: (____)_____

Sales tax:
Please add 7.75% for books shipped to California addresses.   **Tax** _____

Shipping:
$4.00 for the first book and $3.00 for each additional book.   **Shipping** _____

          Total _____

Payment:
( ) Check
( ) Money order
( ) Credit card: ( ) VISA, ( ) Master Card
Do not send cash.

Card number:_____

Name on card: _____ Ex. date_____

Call toll free and order now